Mergers, Acquisitions
and Alternative
Corporate Strategies

Mergers, Acquisitions and Alternative Corporate Strategies
Hill Samuel Bank Limited

Tax: Strategic Corporate Tax Planning
Price Waterhouse

Finance for Growth
National Westminster Bank PLC

Company Law and Competition
S J Berwin & Co

Marketing: Communicating with the Consumer
D'Arcy Masius Benton & Bowles

Information Technology: The Catalyst for Change
PA Consulting Group

Marketing to the Public Sector and Industry
Rank Xerox Limited

Transport and Distribution
TNT Express

Property
Edward Erdman Surveyors

Employment and Training
Blue Arrow PLC

Mergers, Acquisitions
and Alternative Corporate Strategies

Hill Samuel Bank Limited

With a Foreword by
the Rt. Hon. The Lord Young of Graffham
Secretary of State for Trade and Industry

Published in association with
CBI Initiative 1992

MERCURY BOOKS
Published by W.H. Allen & Co. Plc

First published in 1989
by the Mercury Books Division of
W.H. Allen & Co. Plc
Sekforde House, 175–9 St John Street, London EC1V 4LL

Set in Plantin by Phoenix Photosetting, Chatham
Printed and bound in Great Britain by
Mackays of Chatham PLC, Letchworth, Herts

British Library Cataloguing in Publication Data

Mergers, acquisitions and alternative corporate
  strategies.
  1. European community countries. Companies. Mergers.
  Management aspects 2. European Community countries.
  Companies. Acquisitions. Practical information
  I. Hill Samuel. Firm   II. Confederation of British
  Industry
  658.1′6

ISBN 1–85251–012–9

Contents

Foreword

Last year I launched a battle to prepare British business for the single market. Before our 'Europe Open for Business' campaign, very few business men and women had woken up to the single market challenge. Now over 90 per cent of firms are aware of the significance of the single market.

This year the battle is for action. Our weekly survey of business shows that among firms with 100 or more employees nearly 60 per cent are considering what action they need to take to meet the single market challenge.

So British business is on the move. We need to ensure that more firms work out the key issues for their business. That is the main object of our campaign in the months to come.

As the single market is completed, the European Community is becoming our home market. Firms will need to make a basic change in outlook. They will need to get used to the full range of business options. Mergers and acquisitions, joint ventures and local investment need to be considered alongside the option of traditional exporting.

Many UK companies have already taken this message on board. The number of cross-border EC mergers is increasing. UK companies are playing a prominent role in this activity. In the year to September 1988, UK companies made 167 cross-border acquisitions in the EC, with a total value of about £1.5 billion. In the same twelve-month period, companies from the rest of the EC made eighteen cross-border mergers and acquisitions in the UK, with a value of just over £1 billion.

European mergers control is the subject of much interest in this country and in the other member states, and in Brussels where discussions have taken place over the past year on the Commission's proposals for an EC Merger Control Regulation. These can be expected to continue in 1989.

The proposed regulation is of course only one aspect of current Community interest in the whole field of mergers and acquisitions. One important area which it does not address are the barriers, which are more extensive in some member states than in others, to mounting successful *contested* takeovers.

Such barriers can help entrench sluggish management and they spoil the dynamics of capital markets. This is not compatible with the completion of the single market. We are not alone in Europe in our uneasiness. That is why the Commission and other member states supported our initiative at the end of last year on the need to agree a range of action on this front.

The Commission have also formally submitted a Directive on takeovers which is designed to regulate the market conduct of the parties to takeovers.

A lot more discussion can be expected on all these measures. There is a great deal of activity and interest in this area. I doubt if it will slow down. Businesses now recognise that it is time for them to be addressing the issues in detail and considering what action they need take. I congratulate Hill Samuel and CBI Initiative 1992 on the lead which they are giving.

The Rt. Hon. The Lord Young of Graffham,
Secretary of State for Trade and Industry

Preface

Hill Samuel has a long-standing commitment to business in Continental Europe and we were delighted to become one of the ten founder members of CBI Initiative 1992.

This book attempts to draw out the more significant detailed implications for business of 1992 and to offer some insights into how these implications may affect companies' own strategic thinking and subsequent actions. Our approach has been to illuminate generalisation by specific example, wherever possible, and to let case studies of how others have tackled or are tackling European markets speak for themselves.

The focus is on practical issues. The aim is to enable senior executives, with the help of a range of examples and real experiences, to draw valid comparisons with their own situation. This is a task which as a merchant bank with a wide variety of clients, and experience of different types of companies, we feel well qualified to fulfil.

This contribution to the CBI's 1992 initiative has been a major commitment on Hill Samuel's part. Many different sections of the bank have contributed in one way or another to the effort. In addition we owe a particularly deep debt of gratitude to the senior executives of the ten companies who contributed the principal case studies for this book. It is their experiences which bring this book to life. We have to thank them not just for the information and time for extended interviews, which they so freely gave, but also for their frankness even when, in one or two cases, their European plans have not worked out as well as they had originally hoped.

With the onset of 1992 the opportunities for British business in Europe are immense but these can be easily lost. The principal lesson which we have drawn is that a major effort will be required by all of us to identify how best to approach the changing competitive environment, to make the right choices and then to prepare and implement the necessary action plans.

Merchant banks have an important role to play in advising companies in what will be a period of enormous change. Their effectiveness will depend on the depth of their own resources and experience. At Hill Samuel we have one of the largest corporate finance operations in the City and a strong and expanding European network of associated businesses. We are ready to help our clients with the challenges which the single market presents to all of us in the UK.

Sir Richard Lloyd,
Chairman, Hill Samuel Bank Limited

Introduction

The progressive creation of a single market in Europe is having a fundamental effect on the business environment. This is a book about corporate responses to the single market, and, in general, comprises information current at 31 December 1988. It is a study of the implications of the 1992 programme for businesses in the UK and the impact of the changes on strategic thinking and action. Corporate agnosticism to these changes is not a competitive option. The time for awareness is over – now it is time for action.

The heart of the book is contained in the middle section on strategy. This considers how companies should go about formulating their European strategies – both how they should approach the task and the issues they must address. We identify the key strategic options and explain the underlying rationale behind each. We evaluate the advantages and disadvantages of various possible routes for expansion, ranging from organic growth and greenfield entry to acquisitions of, and full mergers with, other European companies.

The impact of the 1992 single market programme on the business environment is included as an essential preliminary to this discussion. This covers both its progress to date and likely future development including the implications for different sectors. The impact of the programme on business is assessed in detail with a consideration of how 1992 will affect the chain of business activity – research and development, manufacturing, distribution and marketing, and pricing.

The final section deals with the issues that follow a decision to seek a Continental acquisition. Particular attention focuses on the differences in practice between the UK and other member states – the problems of identifying suitable acquisition targets, the differing regulatory regimes and the varying cultural attitudes towards mergers and acquisitions.

Ten case studies are interspersed between the main sections of the book. These are personal views of senior industrialists, relating their own experiences of developing and implementing strategies in the EC. The case studies provide an insight into many of the issues discussed throughout the book.

The gathering momentum for a single market

The 1992 programme is unique in terms of the breadth of the legislative measures being prepared, the political uncertainties surrounding their implementation and their potentially large impact on the business environment in the Community. The complexity of the programme reflects the multi-faceted nature of the task of creating a single market: not only is this a matter of removing entry barriers to national markets, the aim is also to try to ensure a level playing-field between competitors on such wide-ranging questions as intellectual property and copyright, standards of consumer and environmental protection, the permitted levels of state aid, the removal of discriminatory public procurement practices, and common enforcement of rules. As important however as the particular detail of the measures is the psychological impact of 1992 on business. The business response to 1992 is generating its own momentum and makes the single market a self-fulfilling concept. Corporate mergers and acquisitions, as well as other forms of alliance in the Community, are already on the increase and can be expected to increase further.

What will actually happen?

Political uncertainties surround many aspects of the 1992 programme. The rate of progress so far in implementing the Commission's 1985 White Paper has confounded many sceptics, but major political obstacles to agreement remain on the removal of physical barriers (e.g. border controls) and fiscal barriers (e.g. VAT approximation and excise duty harmonisation). The greatest political impact, however, lies in the removal of the technical barriers – differing standards, regulatory regimes, etc. The steady adoption of the principle of mutual recognition of other member states' accepted standards (the notion that the Community's aim should be the minimum necessary rather than maximum possible harmonisation) permits much faster progress to agreement than once seemed feasible. None the less, major political difficulties remain as a result of opposition from some member states to the Commission's proposals to limit state aid and liberalise public procurement. An unresolved question is whether creation of the single market will lead to a non-discriminatory approach to companies from outside the Community, and how far reciprocity of access to their countries' markets will be insisted upon.

Implications for business

In research and development, state sponsored aid programmes may well increase in scale as concern grows about Europe's competitiveness with the USA and Japan. But 1992 may lead to rationalisation of research effort in sectors such as pharmaceuticals where, for regulatory reasons, many companies have seen a need to locate facilities in each major state. Also, in telecommunications, liberalisation of public procurement will spur cross-border mergers between national champions. Defence is, however, an area where public policies may continue to protect national firms.

Excess capacity will progressively tend to be eliminated where national barriers presently protect domestic suppliers from lower-cost competitors, for example in sectors such as power engineering. Another agent of change in production processes will be the realisation of economies of scale made possible by the removal of technical barriers to trade. Manufacturing facilities will also need to adjust in order to service new cross-border distribution patterns.

The extent of change in marketing and distribution depends principally on the potential for Eurobrands as well as the logistical feasibility of cross-border selling and the acceptability of products in different national markets. This will vary greatly by sector: in financial services, for instance, the Continental banks' strong distribution networks make direct entry to these markets difficult for outsiders.

Pricing is another area of large potential impact. There are wide price differentials for the same classes of goods and services between member states. Some differentials reflect factors which 1992 will largely leave untouched – non-price factors in the purchase decision, cultural preferences and market structures. But, in a sector like pharmaceuticals, harmonisation of pricing could have a major impact on profitability in the industry.

Framing European business strategies

What are the initial steps companies should take in formulating their European strategies? A strategic review needs to be conducted at the highest level. 1992 is not just a marketing issue: its implications cut across the whole of a company's activities and existing organisational structures. Much depends on broad insight and political judgement. Advisers can be of great help – but the company must first assess both its short- and long-term aims.

Detailed understanding of the relevant Community markets is essential. To achieve this, difficulties in collecting data need to be overcome. Key questions are: How fast is a particular market growing? Can niche opportunities be identified in what appear at first sight to be saturated markets? How deep-seated are cultural differences in consumer preference between countries and regions? What is the potential for Eurobranding? What kind of relationships should be established with dealer networks? Key questions like these need to be addressed and the necessary research undertaken.

Identifying the strategic issues

There are several strands of motivation which can be identified as driving UK businesses into corporate activity within the EC. First, the present business trend is to build on strength rather than diversify and this can push companies into geographical expansion within their particular area of expertise rather than venturing into less related businesses at home. Second, many companies recognise that, in increasingly global markets with intensifying competition, the only route to survival especially against US and Japanese players may be to

3

consolidate their position in what they treat as their European home market. Third, economies of scale in research and production can in some industries such as chemicals and telecommunications be achieved through cross-border rationalisation. Fourth, companies see that, by bringing their skills and know-how to existing businesses on the Continent, they can add value. Fifth, the driving force for consolidating a position through acquisition can sometimes be an international brand-marketing strategy. Sixth, UK manufacturers may wish to acquire their continental distributors in order to get nearer their end-customers and assert more control over their markets. A seventh common motive is a desire to reduce exposure to risks by accessing different suppliers and wider markets. Another risk, of course, is that of unwanted takeover. There is no doubt that defensive moves against takeover threats in advance of 1992 have featured large in some recent corporate moves.

Routes for expansion

There are various routes for expansion a company can choose. Greenfield development can be a high risk strategy with significant start-up costs and no guarantee of long-term success. Trading relationships are often favoured and can be useful in preparing the ground for more permanent arrangements. Strategic links through minority equity stakes allow the investing company to have some share in the benefits which its participation in the target will bring. They can be a first step to acquiring full control, a strategy to overcome political or other objections to foreign ownership of domestic industry, or indeed defensive in nature. In joint ventures, with two or more companies agreeing to vest part of their assets in some form of jointly run operation, management control can be a problem. However, they have proved successful where, for example, the alternative would be cut-throat competition, technological co-operation is required or project development costs are otherwise prohibitive. Acquisition or merger is clearly only one of several feasible routes for expansion. Choosing the best route will depend principally on a realistic assessment of managerial capacities, the relative initial cost and the company's strength to withstand losses in the early years.

Identifying a suitable acquisition target

Information sources about companies are more limited than in the UK, despite efforts by EC authorities to upgrade widely differing standards of auditing and financial reporting among member states. Even if these efforts are successful, accounting standards will continue to vary considerably for some time yet. Identifying who are the actual owners of businesses can also prove difficult given variations in shareholder disclosure requirements and the popularity of bearer shares on the continent. In addition the size of the quoted equity markets is much smaller on the continent than in the UK: many more companies are in private and often family ownership and many of the quoted companies are effectively controlled. Another factor is the continuing prevalence of state holdings in companies in some member states despite a growing emphasis on privatisation.

Understanding the regulatory context

An understanding of the regulatory context is essential when considering mergers or acquisitions on the Continent. The Community's role in competition policy, deriving from Articles 85 and 86 of the Treaty of Rome, is presently in a state of flux, though it is clearly an expanding one. Anti-trust rules vary considerably between member states, as does takeover practice. A takeover directive is currently in draft. The most crucial differences, however, are cultural, including the virtual absence of the hostile takeover bid on the Continent and the ability, in a number of member states, for quoted company management to defend itself very effectively.

Doing the deal

Language skills are a great help in cementing social relations but all except fluent linguists should avoid negotiating complex matters except in their native tongue. Good local advisers are essential both in smoothing contracts and in offering professional services. Managing the acquisition should be addressed at an early stage, in particular whether the incumbent management is to be retained and how vendor-managers are to be motivated. The middle management of an acquired company ought to be given a clear idea of its own future. Acquiring companies often bring in a new chief executive to emphasise that a fresh start is being made and almost always make a priority of introducing their own methods of financial control. In principle, wholesale reorganisation should be avoided except where necessary.

In making an approach, buyers should be open about their intentions. This helps build mutual trust and avoids problems later. Moreover, UK buyers, especially those with a market listing, should recognise that private companies may be unfamiliar with the principles of company valuation, and not be used to the disclosure requirements of UK stock exchange rules, let alone accountants' investigations. Cash is the most normal consideration for continental acquisitions, but personal tax considerations sometimes make a share exchange worth considering.

An awareness of the varying practices of industrial relations and different requirements of employment regulations is essential. In many member states, unions and employee representatives have entrenched legal rights, and trades unions and works councils often play a significant role in corporate developments.

To be successful in acquiring Continental companies management must make a major commitment of time and resources both in conducting what can be protracted negotiations, and in terms of public commitment to employees, suppliers, customers and creditors. In a nutshell, the key ingredients for making successful acquisitions on the Continent are careful preparation, endless patience and a willingness to persist.

I

IMPACT

1. The gathering momentum

What is 1992?

1992 is shorthand for the target date of 31 December 1992 by which member states of the European Community will have implemented a programme of legislation to create a barrier-free internal market. The achievement of this political deadline has been given added momentum by the passing of the Single European Act, which came into force in 1987. This removed the need for unanimity on many of the necessary measures.

Treaty of Rome

This legislative programme is designed to help fulfil one of the key aims of the Treaty of Rome – the creation of a 'Common Market': 'The Community shall have as its task, by establishing a common market and progressively approximating the economic policies of member states, to promote throughout the Community a harmonious development of economic activities, a continuous and balanced expansion, an increase in stability, an accelerated raising of the standard of living and closer relations between the states belonging to it.' In 1985 the European Commission issued a White Paper listing some 300 measures (subsequently reduced to 279) necessary to bring this about.

The sheer breadth of the measures under consideration makes them difficult to grasp. The Commission has identified many barriers to a true single market. These include frontier controls, tax rates, technical standards, national procurement policies, state aid and the inability in some business sectors for firms based in one member state to establish themselves and trade freely in other member states. In some key areas the Commission has yet to produce detailed legislative proposals and there are known to be strong differences of view within the Commission itself. Indeed, in some cases, agreement may prove possible only in a form radically modified from the Commission's original proposal.

Potential effects of legislation

However, the UK's experience in the 1980s has already illustrated how a series of legislative changes can, in combination, have a much greater impact than the individual importance of each might suggest. The last decade has witnessed a transformation of the UK business environment by a series of step-by-step changes. These have included four separate measures of trades union reform; the abolition of controls over wages, prices, borrowing and foreign exchange; tax reforms to increase incentives; and individual privatisations.

In a similar way, the single market legislative programme and the accompanying political commitment is creating a major change in European business psychology. It is already leading companies to think and plan on a European basis – both in seeking business opportunities and in responding to competitive pressures. The programme is generating a momentum whereby it is becoming self-fulfilling.

The political commitment

For most of the 1980s, the economic growth of the EC as a whole has lagged behind that of the USA and Japan. There has also been a significant increase in competition in markets worldwide as a result of the rapid growth of the newly industrialised countries, especially on the Pacific Rim.

New economic policies

At the same time, governments throughout the EC have been losing faith in interventionist solutions to perceived economic weaknesses. This is not just a feature of political change. In France and Spain socialist governments have emphasised the importance of market-orientated policies. Privatisation is becoming more fashionable, even in Italy where the state sector has in the past played a dominant role in industry. The prevailing political climate now favours a much greater reliance on open market competition.

Single European Act

This is demonstrated in the EC by the progress towards the single market. The commitment of the member states' governments was reflected in the passing of the Single European Act, which streamlines decision making in the EC. The key Clause 100 states: 'The Council shall, acting by a qualified majority on a proposal from the Commission in co-operation with the European Parliament and the Economic and Social Committee, adopt the measures for the approximation of the provisions laid down by law, regulation or administrative action in member states which have as their object the establishment and functioning of the internal market. [This] shall not apply to fiscal provisions, to those relating to the free movement of persons nor to those relating to the rights and interests of employed persons.'

The limitations on majority voting are important, but not overwhelming. A key means by which the Commission is hoping to cut

Mutual recognition through delay and complexity is the acceptance of the principle of mutual recognition. The significance of this is plain: instead of the Commission's previous painstaking attempts at universal harmonisation, a standard that has gained approval in one member state will be valid in all the rest. How far it is possible to apply this principle in practice is discussed later, but the switch from the notion of the maximum possible uniformity to the minimum necessary is of central importance. It makes rapid progress more attainable.

Nature of the programme

Some basic conditions must be fulfilled if a single market, undistorted by artificial barriers, is to be created. There must be freedom to enter markets regardless of national boundaries and equal treatment of all the competitors within the markets. In addition there must be:

- Common methods of coping with the shortcomings of the market mechanism, in such areas as consumer and environmental protection, and protection of intellectual property rights
- Compatible, if not common, regulatory mechanisms
- Enforcement of rules in a consistent way across the Community

The creation of a barrier-free market will be no simple matter. The conditions that need to be satisfied for a single market to operate are perhaps best shown by example. The experiences of two key industries – insurance and road haulage – provide good illustrations.

Insurance

Under a Directive passed in 1975 insurance companies were given the freedom to establish themselves in other member states. In practice, however, they are not able to sell the policies they market in their own country freely in other member states because separate regulatory approval has to be sought in each country. This requirement will now be abolished for general insurance of large risks but remains for mass risks and all life assurance.

A free market in insurance is not, however, just a question of each

Consumer protection

member state recognising the validity of the others' approval procedures. Principles of consumer protection vary considerably. In the UK there is provision for a common fund to reimburse policy-holders should insurance companies fail. West Germany regards this as a moral hazard for insurers, encouraging companies to cut corners and take risks. Policy-holders there are protected by elaborate rules on what kind of policies are permissible – setting down firm principles for the actuarial practices on which policies must be based. Compared with the UK, there is closer regulation over how funds can be invested. It is clear, therefore, that unless agreement on the basic principles of consumer protection can be reached, a single market in all types of insurance may prove unattainable.

Road haulage

Quotas

Traditionally, road haulage has been a highly regulated sector where member states have applied quota systems in order to encourage the carriage of freight on the railways. As road freight gradually increased in importance from the late 1960s, Continental countries which were through-routes for long distance transport (particularly West Germany) maintained their road haulage quotas in order to bolster the position of their domestic hauliers. This has been a market, like air transport, with no free entry.

The July 1988 Council of Ministers' decision to phase out bilateral quotas for journeys between member states was a major step in securing free entry for EC road hauliers to all Community markets. Entry will not, however, be completely free until the Community also

Cabotage

succeeds in abolishing existing restrictions on cabotage – the freedom, for example, for a British road haulier to carry goods from West Germany to France after taking a load to West Germany before returning home.

However, even if freedom of entry is established, a level playing-field does not necessarily follow. Road taxes on lorries vary a great deal between member states, although the Commission has made proposals on how these might be put on a common basis. Equally, road haulage is only one mode of physical distribution. As long as some EC countries subsidise rail freight far more than others, there will still remain an important distortion in the freight distribution market place.

Lorry standards

Fortunately, lorry standards throughout the Community have been harmonised in the last ten to fifteen years. These standards address such matters as maximum height and weight, their noise levels and exhaust emissions, the frequency of safety checks and regulation of drivers' hours. Regulation is necessary to protect the public against the consequences of unbridled competition but without this harmonisation a free market would have been an unrealistic target.

The effect on the business environment

It is crucial to understand the mechanisms through which the efficiency gains of a single market will be realised. The removal of barriers, while reducing costs, also reduces market protection. This will obviously lead to a more competitive environment. At the same time, the potential for achieving economies of scale increases as a result of being able to sell more freely to a larger market. Larger markets may bring new sales opportunities, but they also increase pressure on management capabilities.

Increased competition

The benefits of 1992 come about by increasing competitive pressure. There are bound to be losers as well as winners. But it is not a zero-sum game. Lower prices resulting from intensified competition raise consumer purchasing power in real terms. They also increase the Community's competitiveness *vis-à-vis* the rest of the world. Economic estimates of the additional growth the 1992 programme will generate are necessarily speculative. In 1988, a report on the so-called 'costs of non-Europe' was prepared for the Commission. In this study by Paolo Cecchini and his working party, estimates were made of the benefits which could be anticipated if the various barriers to full trade within the Community were dismantled. The results were presented in the form of savings which could be achieved by the removal of all these barriers. The Cecchini study estimated the benefit as a once and

Community GDP

for all boost to Community GDP of between 6.5 per cent and 7.5 per cent. But this calculation is made on the basis that the 1992 programme will be implemented in full; that there are no adverse factors, such as a US recession or oil crisis; and that complementary macro-economic policies are adopted in order to maximise the gains of market integration.

Even though the basis for Cecchini's calculations is unlikely to be fully realised, 1992 will be a positive force for growth in the Community. Moreover, as we have seen in the UK in the 1980s, no economic forecast fully takes account of the dynamic benefits of a change in business psychology. That changing psychology is already evident, and should continue to gather momentum.

The corporate response

The effect on the business environment of the 1992 programme is already acting as a catalyst for change. Increasingly, companies are developing strategies for the single market. Corporate activity is on the increase, with a growing number of cross-border mergers and acquisitions and other types of corporate alliance.

Acquisitions activity Tables 1 and 2 show that the total number of EC cross-border acquisitions more than doubled from 1984 to 1987, increasing by

Table 1: Cross-border activity (buyers) from 1984 to 1987					
Country	1984	1985	1986	1987	% change
Belgium/Luxb'g	0	20	13	13	—
Denmark	12	16	19	11	−8
France	29	36	75	121	+317
Italy	9	14	23	41	+356
Netherlands	35	40	57	80	+129
Spain	7	17	16	15	+114
UK	68	76	92	142	+109
West Germany	49	31	68	72	+47
Total	209	250	363	495	+137

SOURCE: *Acquisitions Monthly*

Table 2: Cross-border activity (sellers) from 1984 to 1987					
Country	1984	1985	1986	1987	% change
Belgium/Luxb'g	11	8	13	38	+245
Denmark	7	4	17	12	+71
France	36	48	72	102	+183
Italy	24	15	26	51	+113
Netherlands	19	17	23	35	+84
Portugal	38	46	56	20	−47
Spain	14	17	24	50	+257
UK	18	39	56	62	+244
West Germany	42	56	76	125	+198
Total	209	250	363	495	+137

SOURCE: *Acquisitions Monthly*

about 100 each year. Companies in some countries, notably the UK, have consistently been far more active as buyers throughout this period. Recently, French and Italian companies in particular have increased their acquisition activity. Buying activity has mainly focused on France and West Germany. More recently, southern Europe has attracted greater interest. As can be seen from Table 3, companies in France, West Germany and the Netherlands have been most active in acquiring UK companies.

Non-EC companies have also stepped up their acquisition activity in the EC but not at the same rate. It is interesting to note from Table 4 that North American buying activity, while predominant, has

Table 3: Acquisitions of UK companies by companies from other EC member states					
Country	1984	1985	1986	1987	1988*
Belgium & Luxembourg	0	0	0	4	2
Denmark	6	6	9	3	1
France	3	10	16	23	17
Italy	0	3	7	3	1
Netherlands	7	12	12	12	6
Portugal	0	0	0	0	—
Spain	0	3	0	0	—
West Germany	2	5	12	17	6
Total	18	39	56	62	33†

* To 1 November
— Figures unavailable
† Excluding Portugal and Spain

SOURCE: *Acquisitions Monthly*

Table 4: Acquisitions within the EC by non-EC companies					
Country	1984	1985	1986	1987	1988*
Norway, Sweden & Finland	46	96	41	81	42
Switzerland & Austria	36	52	76	93	32
USA & Canada	151	172	143	160	54
Other (including Japan)	38	66	74	88	43
Total	271	386	334	422	171

* To 1 November 1988

SOURCE: *Acquisitions Monthly*

shown little change in recent years. Countries from other parts of Europe and the Far East have become more active. However groundless the fears of 'Fortress Europe', such moves represent an insurance policy for companies against an adverse change in the political climate towards protectionism.

These trends underline the pace of change in the Community. EC companies are moving to position themselves in what they now regard as their domestic European market – one which will be more open and at the same time more competitive. Real political commitment has already been demonstrated and a far-reaching single market programme is being implemented.

The removal of internal barriers will boost economic growth throughout the EC. The effect of this on the business environment, together wth the liberalisation of markets and mutual recognition or harmonisation of standards, will have an impact of unprecedented scale and complexity. The opportunities for business depend on the ability of management to grasp what is happening and how it affects their particular business.

2. What will actually happen?

Implementation of the programme

The rate of progress of the 1992 programme has taken most observers by surprise. By the end of 1988, the Council of Ministers had already adopted around 40 per cent of the measures in the 1985 EC White Paper. Of the remainder, more than half were before the Council.

While it is undoubtedly true that many of the easiest subjects have been tabled first, the Community has several major achievements to its credit, which include:

- Agreement on the phased abolition of all capital controls
- The Single Administrative Document simplifying frontier procedures for cross-border freight
- Phased elimination of bilateral quotas in road haulage
- Liberalisation of large risk general insurance, such as oil rigs and airliners (as opposed to mass risks, where questions of consumer protection in areas like household and motor insurance make progress more difficult)
- Permission for unit trusts authorised in one member state to operate on the mutual recognition principle in other member states, though still subject to national rules on marketing practice

The Commission's own presentation of the 1992 programme identifies three types of barrier:

- Physical barriers, such as controls at frontiers, passport checks, agricultural and health checks, and restrictions on cross-border methods of transport
- Fiscal barriers, such as VAT rates and excise duties
- Technical barriers, such as differing technical standards, and the lack of a common market for services and open tendering for public contracts

This brings to the fore two of the classes of measure to which the Commission itself attaches particular importance – the abolition of physical controls at frontiers and the harmonisation of VAT and excise duties. However, it is already clear that these proposals face major political obstacles, in addition to requiring the unanimous agreement of the member states.

Physical barriers

Opposition to removal of frontier checks

While supporting the principle of reducing physical barriers, the UK government has opposed the abolition of some frontier checks on the grounds that their full removal will inhibit the fight against terrorism and drug-trafficking. There are increasing indications that this concern is widely shared by public opinion in the Community. The only way progress towards the complete abolition of frontier checks can be made is by achieving visible, enhanced co-operation between national law enforcement agencies.

The removal of all frontier controls is, in fact, a relatively small part of the 1992 programme. The cost of physical delays at frontiers was estimated in the Cecchini Report at between 1.5 per cent and 2 per cent of the value of each consignment, or 4 to 7 per cent of the total costs which could be saved if the 1992 programme were implemented in full. The introduction of the Single Administrative Document will go some way to achieving these savings. Moreover, it may be possible to save on the costs of frontier delays by streamlining procedures without removing checks altogether – by, for instance, having checks carried out at only one border control point rather than both (as has already been agreed).

Fiscal barriers

VAT

The UK has been the most outspoken of all the member states in its opposition to the Commission's proposals on VAT approximation. However, other member states which face the problem of severe loss of tax revenues if VAT rates are approximated downwards (as can be seen from Table 5) may privately welcome the UK's willingness to take a high profile stance on this issue. There are signs, at the time of writing, that the Commission may be prepared to change its proposals to introduce minimum rates rather than tax bands, which may assist the negotiations.

Differential rates of tax on consumer spending lead to few artificial distortions in the location of business activity. This is not true of all forms of taxation – higher corporation taxes may well have an adverse impact on decisions about location. The Treasury, the Institute of Directors and other UK institutions have frequently pointed to the experience of the US single market, where different rates of sales tax apply from state to state. Problems of cross-border shopping may occur in the Community in the short term, but the discipline of the market will, in time, tend to approximate rates between neighbouring tax-setting authorities.

Excise duties

Harmonisation of excise duties is a greater problem. Because the existing divergences are so great, the implications of harmonisation for tax revenues and retail prices in some countries would be dramatic. Cigarettes cost nearly eight times as much in Denmark as they do in Greece: the tax yield on a packet is some eleven times greater. If Greece were to adopt Danish tobacco prices, present Greek cigarette consumption is so high that its retail price index for all goods con-

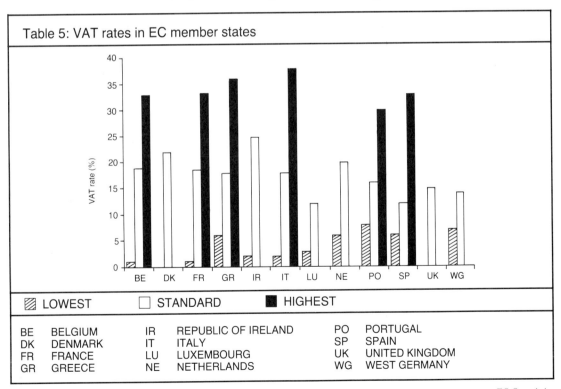

Table 5: VAT rates in EC member states

LOWEST   STANDARD   HIGHEST

BE	BELGIUM	IR	REPUBLIC OF IRELAND	PO	PORTUGAL
DK	DENMARK	IT	ITALY	SP	SPAIN
FR	FRANCE	LU	LUXEMBOURG	UK	UNITED KINGDOM
GR	GREECE	NE	NETHERLANDS	WG	WEST GERMANY

SOURCE: *EC Commission*

sumed would rise by 13 per cent. Yet the chances must be slight that, in the face of strong protests from the north European health lobby, high duty countries like Denmark (and to a lesser extent the UK) will agree to lower their excise duties.

Agreement on alcohol duties may, however, be more feasible. There has been talk of zonal arrangements and extended phasing towards common rates over a long time period. Such a compromise, if implemented, might well have a significant impact on market opportunities for different types of brand and manufacturer.

Technical barriers

Despite the high profile given to abolition of frontier controls and to VAT approximation, the heart of the 1992 programme lies in the potential impact on business of the measures contained in the catch-all category of technical barriers. This is where the principle of mutual recognition holds out the greatest hope of facilitating rapid progress. But even here matters are not as simple as they may seem.

Were the mutual recognition principle to be applied without qualification, then an inevitable result would be a process of competition between different sets of national rules. In this competition the most de-regulated member state would have a considerable advantage. Some fear that standards would in time be forced down to the lowest common denominator. Otherwise, businesses in the most highly regulated countries would be put at a competitive disadvantage.

Because of this obvious danger, there are limitations on the extent to which mutual recognition can be applied without qualification. Harmonisation of standards still remains necessary in such areas as environmental and consumer protection.

Technical standards

Protection through minimum standards
On environmental and health and safety questions, the Single European Act commits the Commission to propose minimum standards which guarantee a high level of protection. In the chemicals industry, for example, far from leading to any averaging down of standards, 1992 is expected to raise them. This may have major consequences for costs. In West Germany, the member state with the strictest environmental laws, about half of total capital expenditure in the next four years will be devoted to environment and safety.

There are areas, however, where the mutual recognition principle will be of great practical application and avoid much time-consuming harmonisation. In future, there will undoubtedly be fewer public arguments about the definition of the European sausage. Products accepted as fit on health and safety grounds for consumption in one country will be freely sold in others. The Community has abandoned attempts to harmonise the content of particular foods as they painstakingly attempted in cases such as natural mineral water, chocolate and honey. Instead, it is concentrating on setting up a framework of minimum standards. These include food labelling and additives, articles in contact with food, and food inspection.

Inspection of foodstuffs

For example, in the case of the inspection of foodstuffs, the Draft Directive aims to standardise legislation for a system of food inspection at specific points in the distribution chain. It covers such areas as frequency of inspection, hygiene standards, standards of competence for inspectors and analytical test procedures. Mutual recognition eases, therefore, rather than eliminates, the need for harmonisation. Fears that it will lead to a dramatic lowering of acceptable standards of environment, safety and consumer protection are much exaggerated.

Financial services

In financial services, mutual recognition will not be allowed to override national concerns for consumer protection. For example, unit trusts authorised in any one member state can now be marketed in any other. National marketing rules must, however, still be adhered to on such matters as permissible methods of cold-calling, the content of newspaper advertising, information that must be disclosed to customers, and the rights of customers to withdraw from contracts.

The Draft Second Banking Directive proposes home country regulation in order to facilitate the operation of a single banking licence for the Community as a whole. But this is tempered by the proposal that host state regulatory agencies can intervene where considerations of the public good are at stake. This may, for instance, permit the UK to apply parts of the Financial Services Act to Continental banks operating in the UK if the consumer protection requirements of their home country regulators are less stringent.

Insurance

In insurance, widely differing actuarial practices, as well as national variations in the rules on permitted investments, are all argued to be in the interests of consumer protection. It is generally expected that, in the life insurance field, this will effectively prevent any real progress towards mutual recognition. In general insurance, there may be an opening up in the area of mass risks, as a follow-up to the agreed Second Insurance Directive in 1988 on large risks, though this cannot be done without agreement on minimum standards of consumer protection – a concern that an important judgment of the European Court upheld.

Open tendering for public contracts

Defence

An area where political pressures may make it difficult to realise the full benefits of 1992 is public procurement. This is particularly so in defence procurement, where governments may continue to seek to retain a national supplier in each of the major equipment markets. Most member states consider defence to lie outside the ambit of the Treaty of Rome in any event.

Obstacles to rationalisation

Redundancy fears in industries with problems of gross over capacity, and which are heavily dependent on public purchasing, may make it difficult to achieve the necessary rationalisation. A recent study for the European Commission suggested that, in the case of power station boiler manufacturers, firms in the EC were working at only 20 per cent capacity. Opening up the public procurement market in this area was forecast to lead to a reduction in company numbers from fifteen to four. Yet governments are unwilling to put their own national champions at risk, particularly when the manufacturing plant is located in an area of high unemployment.

In some areas, liberalisation of public procurement seems likely to proceed fairly quickly. The planned doubling of the Community's Regional and Social Funds represents a large increase in the finance available for major infrastructure projects, particularly in Portugal and other parts of southern Europe. As these are Community programmes, albeit with matching national finance, the Commission can effectively insist that tendering is genuinely open. Public expenditure pressures on health services throughout the Community, coupled with strong consumer demand for the best available treatment, may well increase member states' willingness to purchase equipment and supplies, including pharmaceuticals, from the cheapest possible source.

In certain areas, liberalisation of public procurement may well be gradual, giving domestic suppliers time to adjust, and may involve, as a condition, some acceptance of discrimination against non-EC suppliers. In telecommunications network equipment, AT&T and Canada's Northern Telecom are strongly placed to compete with EC suppliers. In Italy and Spain, where domestic producers are technologically weak, there may be less resistance to purchasing from the best available suppliers, even if these are not EC companies. But in France, West Germany and the UK, the practice of protecting domestic suppliers – Alcatel, Siemens and GEC/Plessey, respectively – through public purchasing arrangements is well ingrained.

The protection of these markets for the national supplier was one of the key reasons behind Siemens' link-up with GEC in their joint bid for Plessey. The aim was to leave Siemens with 40 per cent of GPT, the

GEC/Plessey telecommunications switching joint venture. For Siemens this may represent the only way into this UK market, given that British Telecom has confined its switching orders to GEC/Plessey's 'System X' and, to a lesser extent, Ericsson's 'System Y'.

The liberalisation of public procurement touches on a central, outstanding question of the 1992 programme – attitudes to non-EC companies and trading relationships with the rest of the world. The dilemmas have shown up most acutely in the case of cars. In particular, the UK and France have clashed over whether the Nissan Bluebird, produced in Sunderland, can be regarded as a European car and therefore not subject to quotas on imports into the Community.

Import restrictions

It may seem that 1992 is an opportunity to eliminate all existing import restrictions, but this view is not universally shared. A major unresolved issue is whether, and in what form, Japanese voluntary export restraints will apply to the single market as a whole, rather than individual national markets. Moreover, local content rules to be applied by the Commission need to be ageed in respect of 'screwdriver' plants set up by Far East producers in the EC because of limitations on their direct exports.

The decision-making process

Despite the significant progress in the programme to date, the Commission's proposals will not be implemented in their entirety. If companies are to plan effectively, they need to form a view of what, in fact, is likely to happen. Understanding the complexity of the Community's decision-making processes is an essential first step.

Draft legislation readily available

Brussels is a much more open political community than Whitehall. Normally in the UK, draft legislative proposals in their formative stage are kept confidential until a White Paper or Bill is published. In the Community, drafts are widely available. All interested parties can make their views known, if they take the necessary time and trouble. In this open system, there is a complex process of continual compromise involving the separate interests of the twelve member states, the far from monolithic views of the Community institutions and lobbying by a variety of interest groups. The European Parliament plays an increasingly important role.

Value of lobbying

Within the Brussels village, a company that has a strong case to make, and knows how to lobby, has a good chance of making its influence felt and having its legitimate interests taken into account.

Companies should, however, appreciate that all the member states are locked into a process of continuous bargaining. The more one member state raises the profile of a particular matter, the more likely it will feel the need to give ground on other matters in order to prove that it is behaving in a '*communautaire*' way.

Although not all the Commission's targets will be achieved, the general goal of market integration has secured widespread acceptance. Increasingly the general goal will override what, in the past, have proved obstinate special interests.

From this discussion three general conclusions can be drawn:

- The purpose of 1992 is to break down barriers to a single market: the higher those barriers in any sector, the greater will be the impact of the 1992 programme on that sector

- How much of the programme will be implemented is uncertain: political factors will, in some sectors (such as public procurement), have a critical influence on the impact of 1992

- The programme will have wider effects than the direct consequences of the proposed measures themselves: the catalytic effect on business psychology will itself generate momentum for change.

3. Implications for business

Each company needs to work out the implications of the 1992 programme for its own activities. The implications will vary by sector as well as by individual circumstance but, clearly, many companies that have traditionally only been exporters to the Continent will be considering whether their approach is adequate for future commercial needs.

This chapter examines the impact of the 1992 programme in the following key areas of business activity:

- Research and development (R&D)

- Manufacturing

- Marketing and distribution

- Pricing

Research and development

In pharmaceuticals, many of the big companies have established research facilities in each principal member state. They have seen practical advantages in having a research presence in each country in order to ease the task of dealing with the national regulatory authorities. At present each country has its own separate national approval procedures for licensing new drugs. These are frequently onerous and time-consuming. The thrust of the 1992 programme is towards either mutual recognition of differing national standards or a centralised approval procedure at Community level, or some combination of the two. As a result, the political need for locating research centres in each country may be much diminished. It may become feasible to realise economies of scale through rationalisation of research.

In some industries, the pattern of R&D may change as a result of the restructuring of EC industry which the dynamics of 1992 will stimulate. The development costs of the next generation of public switching equipment are expected to be huge. It was these pressures that led the long-standing British rivals, GEC and Plessey, to combine their tele-communications operations in the GPT joint venture agreed in 1987. However, the size of market necessary to justify long-term R&D investment is well beyond that of even the largest member state. In a single European market, many observers expect only one or possibly two EC players to survive. Once public procurement is opened up, market forces can be expected to produce rapid concentration in some industries.

Rationalisation in key sectors

Liberalisation of public procurement will therefore lead to a rationalisation of R&D effort in certain key sectors. But a factor which may inhibit full achievement of critical R&D mass is the continuance of national policies in defence procurement.

Traditionally, defence ministries have sought, on national security grounds, to maintain national suppliers in each main equipment market. Nevertheless, for some years, cost pressures have led to an increasing emphasis on collaborative arrangements. Unfortunately these have not always proved cost-effective. The only practical altern-ative is to buy American and, in some cases, such as the Boeing/AWACS versus GEC/NIMROD argument in the UK, governments have been prepared to do this. Defence decision-makers may increas-ingly come to the conclusion that, in many spheres, their only realistic choice is between facilitating the creation of a single, efficient European supplier, or buying from the USA.

Defence ministries may now look more benevolently on cross-border mergers and joint ventures in the defence sector than they have in the past. A good example of this changed atmosphere is the recent merger of two computer systems businesses – CAP of the UK, and Sema Metra of France – to form the new Sema Group. Those com-panies were heavily engaged in defence-related work, and yet both governments were prepared to allow the merger, notwithstanding the defence contracts.

Manufacturing

In a single market the pattern of manufacturing will alter considerably as a result of:

- Elimination of excess capacity where national barriers are protecting domestic suppliers from lower-cost competition

- Realisation of economies of scale as products which are now required to meet different national specifications can be sold throughout the Community

- Consequences for manufacturing of any reorganisation of distribution which the dismantling of frontier barriers may facilitate, such as plant location

Excess capacity

Excess capacity can be dealt with first. Markets with the highest excess capacity are likely to be those that have been protected by discriminatory national procurement policies. It is possible that many capital goods industries selling mainly to governments or public utilities are to some extent in this exposed position.

Cars

Technical standards are a more generalised barrier to trade. The car industry is a good example of how removal of technical standards may alter the manufacturing pattern in a far-reaching way. The lack of a single EC-wide approval procedure requires costly and time-consuming duplication and, for example, varying exhaust emission standards still apply, although common agreement has now been reached. There are also unique national vehicle equipment requirements, such as side repeater flasher lights in Italy, dim-dip lighting in the UK, yellow headlamps in France, and reclining driver's seats and separate rear reflectors in West Germany.

These barriers (along with other trade and fiscal barriers) affect the production process by limiting the maximum feasible production run for each basic model of car. As a result the average costs of production are considerably higher than they would be in a single market.

One of the sector studies carried out for the Cecchini report estimates that, as a result of the single market, the number of separate vehicle platforms produced within the EC would fall from 30 to 21. (A platform is a single vehicle manufacturing module, which can be varied in length to permit model variants.) In turn, within the same total production, the volume per platform will rise considerably. These are the first round static effects. The dynamic effects would show up later in increased competitiveness *vis-à-vis* imports from outside the EC and an expansion in home demand due to lower prices. At the same time, the components manufacturers will be able to take advantage of much higher production runs as long as they can sell at competitive prices to the car makers who will survive.

Building materials

In building materials, bulkiness of transport is not as big a natural barrier to cross-border trade as might be supposed, even though the transport costs of some materials are high. The reality is that French and West German technical standards are extremely difficult for outsiders to meet. The 1992 programme is attempting to harmonise essential safety standards but leave other product approval procedures to mutual recognition. This will encourage an opening-up of markets to different types of products.

This development is expected to be favourable to UK companies who tend to be much larger than their Continental rivals in this sector. But prospects for UK expansion in Continental markets will be limited by the extent to which differing standards are features of costly infrastructure which cannot be standardised quickly.

Against this background, UK building materials companies may well pursue cautious strategies. These could include increasing exports from the UK; the establishment of greenfield facilities, particularly in southern Europe, where the construction market is growing fast but where transport costs are particularly high; and the acquisition of smaller EC producers in less developed markets, whose products they could add to their range and whose local presence they can use to good advantage for marketing and distribution purposes.

Food

The Commission's new approach to removing barriers in the food sector has already been described – with harmonisation agreed on core issues such as product labelling and packaging, additives and adhesive wrappings, together with mutual recognition of any product judged fit for human consumption by the authorities in one member state.

The UK appears, in principle, to be in a strong position in this sector, with many sizeable and successful companies that ought to be able to take advantage of a single market once the technical barriers are removed. However, with some notable exceptions, few UK companies have so far established much of a continental presence.

Marketing and distribution

Eurobrands or cross-border selling

The food sector also provides a good example of the possible consequences for manufacturing of marketing and distribution changes brought about by 1992. Food is a fast-moving consumer commodity where Eurobrands can readily be established. At present, companies with a presence throughout the EC, like Unilever, tend to manufacture in each local market. The logic of this approach may be eroded once non-tariff barriers are removed and road haulage liberalised, with frontier barriers reduced to the point where journeys across borders are not significantly more costly, mile for mile, than journeys within national boundaries. It may then become logistically more efficient, for example, to service supermarkets in Benelux, the Rhineland and South East England (once the Channel Tunnel is built) from a plant in northern France.

Data transmission

This illustration is a good example of the inter-relationships of 1992. The efficient production and distribution of fast-moving consumer goods is dependent on the effective transmission of information collected at the point of sale. A possible constraint is whether reliable data networks can be established across frontiers. The incompatibilities between the managed data networks operated by national, usually publicly owned, telephone operators could present a serious obstacle.

Dealer networks

For other manufactured products, the main concern may be how 1992 will affect established distribution channels. Many manufacturers sell through dealer networks which in practice have partitioned the market between them. As a result, price differences can be quite significant between markets. With mutual recognition of products, there will be little to stop dealers, or agents, crossing borders in order to take advantage of the price differences. Where products require after-sales service, such activity could upset established arrangements and damage product reputations in the process as well as cause difficulties in handling warranty claims. To resolve this problem, manufacturers could acquire the dealers themselves in order to establish control. Alternatively, they may encourage the dealers to combine, but at the risk that this may strengthen the dealers' negotiating hand in pricing discussions with the manufacturer. A different approach would be to enter into an arrangement with a complementary manufacturer in another member state, with its own dealer network or direct sales force through which the company's products can be sold.

Unit trusts

In financial services, access to distribution is the key to the opening up of the market, even if regulatory liberalisation is satisfactorily achieved. In the unit trust sector, it is conceivable that the UK industry may attempt direct entry. It can draw on its own well-developed strengths in the design, advertising and direct mail selling of unit trusts, though it will still have to ensure that its methods comply with local marketing rules in each member state. How far direct entry is a viable strategy depends crucially on marketing practice as well as differing national rules.

However, in financial services generally, banks have very strong distribution networks, which are used for selling a wide variety of financial products. The strength of these existing networks makes direct entry difficult, even if mutual recognition of home country regulation technically permits it. Only the largest players are likely to consider direct entry. Acquisitions, joint ventures and trading relationships therefore appear more likely.

Pricing

Some of the most serious consequences of 1992 may be on existing pricing policies and profitability. At present there are considerable price differentials within the EC, particularly between the UK and other member states. A common assumption is that 1992 will eliminate these price differentials or at least erode them to the point where only cost differences, such as varying transport charges, can account for them.

Differentials   Price differentials must, however, be seen in the context of a much wider picture. Some detailed research on differentials between the UK and the rest of the EC has been undertaken by the Henley Centre for Forecasting. Table 6 shows the results of this analysis in those sectors where prices in the UK were at least 15 per cent higher or lower than in the rest of the EC. It also shows import penetration, the proportion of production exported and Henley's own estimate of

Table 6: Price differences and trade performances				
Product	UK Price[1]	Imports[2]	Exports[3]	Degree of barriers[4]
Glassware & tableware	+41.3	30	24	L
Wine & cider	+25.1	72	12	M
Motor vehicles, cycles & motor-cycles	+22.0	51	34	M
Mining equipment	+20.0	3	14	H
Metalworking machine tools	+18.8	40	35	H
Mineral water, non-alcoholic beverages	+15.7	13	3	L
Machinery for food, chemicals, rubber	−18.4	61	66	H
Liqueurs & spirits	−18.6	54	88	L
Beer	−21.8	5	4	H
Newspapers, periodicals, other printed materials	−23.9	2	3	L
Chocolate & confectionery	−32.2	15	11	H

SOURCE: *Henley Centre*

[1] Percentage difference between the UK and average Community price (+indicates UK price higher)
[2] Import penetration measured by imports as a proportion of home demand
[3] Export penetration measured by exports as a proportion of domestic manufactures
[4] Estimated degree of trade barriers H(High), M(Medium), L(Low)

whether the technical barriers to trade are low, medium or high. From this analysis, it emerges that price differentials can be very large. Glassware and tableware is over 40 per cent more expensive in the UK than in the rest of the EC; chocolate and confectionery over 30 per cent cheaper.

Price differentials cannot always be easily explained. At first sight they represent potential new business opportunities which companies contemplating market entry ought to examine. But it is naive to believe that 1992 will sweep all differentials away because they have various causes:

- Non-price factors such as reliability and after-sales services can be crucial in the decision to purchase

- Price itself is regarded for some products as an indicator of quality, often reinforced by brand image

- Cultural influences often explain varying consumer preferences and differences in taste

- Market structures can impede entry for cheaper products

- Market dominance may deter new entrants

Cultural factors   Of these, the importance of cultural factors should not be under-estimated: Belgians prefer Belgian chocolate to Quality Street, even though Rowntree's products may be a lot cheaper; in mortgage products people in other member states appear to have a strong preference for the fixed rate mortgage: they prefer the certainty of knowing the extent of their commitments to the uncertainty of the standard UK variable-rate product. The thrust of this argument is that pricing will not necessarily be subject to dramatic change, although considerable rewards will go to those who can spot the opportunities.

It follows that every company needs to analyse the nature of its business to be able fully to appreciate the likely impact of the single market changes. Only then will it be possible to focus on the right strategy to take advantage of the new opportunities and avoid the pitfalls which will occur.

CASE STUDY

Castrol
Long-term growth through consistent acquisition strategies

Report of an interview with Jonathan Fry, Chief Executive

Castrol is one of the world's largest and most successful marketers of lubricants in all their forms. It accounts for some 80 per cent of Burmah Oil's present business. For Castrol, Europe is but one region of a UK business that has built up a strong presence worldwide. Currently Castrol is divided into thirty-four operating units selling in some 150 countries.

Yet Continental Europe is an extremely important area of business, accounting for just over a third of Castrol's turnover and nearly half of its total profit. The story of how Castrol has achieved this leading position is worthy of attention for any company contemplating a European-cum-global strategy.

As Jonathan Fry puts it, 'the first thing to appreciate about Castrol is that our position has taken decades to build up'. Castrol started in the 1930s establishing a brand image built on the popularity of motor racing. By the outbreak of the Second World War it had expanded into the old Commonwealth and had subsidiaries in several of the main Continental countries. None the less in the 1960s 80 per cent of the business was still focused on the UK.

In the last twenty-five years, Castrol has gradually been strengthening its position in a piecemeal but consistent way. Most acquisitions have followed a familiar pattern. Castrol has entered new markets in a low-cost way by appointing local distributors. As business has built up, Castrol has then bought them out in order to create its own national marketing subsidiaries.

The most recent instances where this process has occurred have been in the rapidly developing markets of Spain, Portugal and Greece. In Spain, for example, Castrol sales were held back for years due to the effect of import quotas: now these are being relaxed and the market is expanding fast. In both Spain and Greece, Castrol has bought out its distributors fully. In Portugal, however, it has entered into a joint venture because the local distributor proved reluctant to sell 100 per cent of its business. Finland is now the only country in Europe where an independent distributor continues to market Castrol products.

Why has Castrol pursued this strategy? Mainly as a device to consolidate its position in the market place. Through owning the distributor, Castrol is more in control of its own marketing and pricing. It has a greater guarantee of security against new entrants. It is able to exploit to the full Castrol's powerful brand image. Finally, by seeking worldwide coverage and establishing a leading position in most markets, it is able to provide much broader technical and marketing knowledge to its customers, at all levels, in its own particular specialist field.

At the same time Castrol has pursued a strategy of buying related businesses. However, as Jonathan Fry emphasises, 'we have always sought genuine synergy. In Castrol we have always avoided the temptation of acquiring a collection of vaguely related businesses.' The basic criteria for acquisition is that the business has to be in 'lubes' or something very close to it. Castrol bought Simoniz car wax, for example. It has to be a business to which Castrol can apply its marketing skills, preferably exploiting the technology of the company it has acquired on a much grander scale. Acquisition candidates have to be in 'specialist' not 'commodity' businesses.

An obvious question is 'Why has Castrol enjoyed so much success on the acquisition trail?' Jonathan Fry puts it down to a mixture of circumstances and style. 'We've concentrated on niches which are too small for the oil majors and too big for the rest of the competition.' Castrol is in the fortunate position, in most cases, of being a sought-after partner. 'People recognise the potential to "Castrolise" their products by applying our marketing skills and techniques to market them worldwide.'

An example in recent years of this strategy came with the acquisition of Consulta, a metal-working oils business in West Germany. Consulta produces a highly specialist product which had hardly been marketed beyond a fifty-mile radius of the plant. Once under Castrol's wing, a much bigger marketing effort could be made. And in terms of branding, the Castrol name could be added as a prefix to that of the locally familiar product.

What does Castrol see as the lessons from its acquisitions record? Jonathan Fry emphasises that Castrol is highly decentralised. In many cases local management has been kept on. There is no other way they feel they could run their far-flung empire. 'We're not in favour of wholesale slaughter once we've made an acquisition.' Castrol might well send in a British expatriate to help out a local chief executive, but not generally to take command. They would also send in an audit team to check on the financial systems, but they have no mobile 'acquisition squad' which tours the world 'sorting out companies Burmah has bought'.

One final lesson which Jonathan Fry emphasised was that 'You have to be patient and you need a deep pocket, as more capital will usually be required to develop the business'.

CASE STUDY

Christian Salvesen
Flexible approaches to building on strength

*Report of an interview with Barry Sealey, Deputy
Chairman and Managing Director*

Barry Sealey regards Continental Europe as an integral part of Christian
Salvesen's business. 'I get very irritated by people who talk about moving
into Europe. Britain has been in Europe since 1973 and Christian Salvesen
now has over a third of its business overseas.' He sees the 1992 programme,
apart from specific sectors such as financial services where big changes are
to be expected, as largely symbolic. 'It's all about making people think
seriously about doing business in the Community.'

Despite the strength of this commitment it was by no means easy for
a business of Christian Salvesen's nature to expand on the Continent.
'For a producer of goods, Europe is relatively open. Manufacturing
companies can think in terms of Europe-wide strategies in respect of
their sales. This is not so for a provider of physical services. Infrastructure has to be built up in the countries where the service is
provided. While we have certain skills and know-how we can apply in
any country, a service provider needs to set up in advance in the
country concerned before it can begin to compete.'

The service Christian Salvesen pre-eminently provides is the distribution of temperature-controlled products which are principally
food-related. Indeed, in the rough, competitive and low margin world
of road haulage, Christian Salvesen has become a major force in this
specialist niche. Success in this area requires the effective planning
and use of cold stores and bulk-break depots as well as management of
a road haulage operation.

As a business it has pursued a strategy of concentrating on what it
does best. This led it to dispose of its housebuilding and seafoods
businesses in recent years. But it still retains a highly profitable
industrial and marine division (accounting for about 20 per cent of
turnover and 30 per cent of profit).

Determination to focus on its strengths led Christian Salvesen into
Continental markets in the first place in 1977. 'We thought we were
running out of expansion opportunities in the UK – quite wrongly as it
turned out. But it was this perception which led us to believe we
should extend our core activities to the continent.' Barry Sealey's view

is that it is better to expand on the Continent in the business you know than diversify in the UK into 'so-called related businesses, where the connections with your own are often quite spurious'.

Because of the need to build up infrastructure, Christian Salvesen has expanded gradually. The 1977 'initial' entry was into France: 'In fact, as close to home as we could possibly get – in Boulogne, where we saw a market opportunity.' Christian Salvesen now has six major operating units in France, all 'greenfield' projects. In addition it has established two greenfield operations in Belgium. But in the Netherlands and West Germany, Christian Salvesen has proceeded by acquisition – buying three companies in the Netherlands between 1984 and 1985 and two in West Germany in 1987. Its latest Continental move is a greenfield entry into Spain. 'Christian Salvesen would like in time to get into Italy as well, probably by acquisition.'

Christian Salvesen has chosen no single method of entry into the European market, and clearly the reasons why its approach has varied according to country are of considerable interest. Essentially its tactics have been strongly influenced by its ability to win contracts in advance of setting up operations. For example, its relationships with Mars in the UK put it in a strong position to bid for a Mars pet food distribution contract in France: it was with that assurance behind it that Christian Salvesen established a greenfield site at Langen, near Bordeaux. Similarly in Belgium, Christian Salvesen obtained a contract before it built a site. This was not too much of a problem because in Belgium there was no effective competition in frozen food distribution. Christian Salvesen's latest move in Spain resulted from a French company, for which it handled distribution, wanting to expand in Spain.

Christian Salvesen has not, however, always waited to win contracts before taking the risk of entry. Its first greenfield site in Boulogne was set up 'because we saw a market opportunity there for a cold store'. In Paris, Christian Salvesen won contracts while its distribution site was under construction. It took these risks because it had confidence in its competitive edge in its main business. 'And anyway,' as Barry Sealey puts it, 'there were no French businesses we thought worth buying.'

In the Netherlands and West Germany circumstances were rather different. There was an over-supply of cold storage, and, as a result, Christian Salvesen ruled out large scale greenfield entry. In the Netherlands it acquired three separate businesses – a cold store, a fresh food distributor and a distributor of tobaccos and wines. In the first two instances it bought businesses with which it was already familiar and where it could apply its own successful techniques.

In West Germany Christian Salvesen acquired two distribution companies, one of which was a subsidiary of Unilever and the other an independent contractor. A good commercial relationship with Unilever was of crucial importance in making those deals. 'In West Germany there are very limited opportunities for greenfield entry. In order to get anywhere fast, we had to make an acquisition and speed was essential given that we wanted to be well positioned to take advantage of the impending deregulation of the West German road haulage industry,' which, according to Barry Sealey, 'has been the most regulated and highly priced in Europe'.

Barry Sealey describes the key requirements for success in Europe as follows:

- It is essential to know the market. 'Every European country is different. For example, in the UK freezer centres have been a great success – but in West Germany 25 per cent of frozen food is delivered direct to the home. Continental countries are as different from each other as from the UK.' The essential need to know the market means that businesses should only make acquisitions in spheres they understand.

- In making an acquisition, local knowledge is essential and in Barry Sealey's words, 'it's got to be your own. Bankers and consultants can be of great help. But they are an add-on, not a substitute for what you must know yourself.'

- Expansion on the Continent requires a great commitment of time. 'You have got to spend enormous amounts of time talking to people and winning their confidence.' Buying businesses is not easy. 'There's a big problem in motivating management, particularly if it's a private, management owned company and, in essence, you're putting a lot of money in the existing management's pocket.' From Christian Salvesen's point of view it is a lot easier to buy subsidiaries of existing big businesses rather than small firms. 'They already understand corporate ways.'

- Once an acquisition is made, Barry Sealey stresses 'the need to take control'. He believes in putting Christian Salvesen's own people into every business Christian Salvesen acquires. That does not mean the local top management is replaced. 'The Salvesen manager might come in as the existing chief's deputy. But when you make an acquisition, people expect change right from the start.' Christian Salvesen managers are not, however, all expatriate British. A Swede runs their German operation, for example. But in France they had management problems until they succeeded in identifying a 'Francophile Brit' who was keen to live in France and run the operation there. 'Of course in the longer term we intend to find suitable French management. But the first requirement was to use someone who understood our business, had our skills and could bridge the language and cultural barrier.'

- A final piece of advice which Barry Sealey emphasises time and again: 'Stick to your last.'

II

STRATEGY

4. Framing a European business strategy

Clearly, something major is happening in the EC, something which will affect every business in the UK to a greater or lesser extent, if the effects are not already being felt. Political action is being taken which could change the nature of both markets and business practices. UK companies' competitors are getting the same messages, and some are already putting in hand responses appropriate to the new conditions. The old protectionist barriers which made it hard for UK businesses to operate on the Continent (and vice versa) are to be removed.

Getting started

A host of corporate advisers are making pronouncements about 1992: how important it is; how we must all be ready, and so on. But where does a company start? First, it must get the internal company processes right by which an effective European business strategy can be developed. Then it must develop an understanding of the substantive issues which will shape that strategy through:

- A cool, hard assessment of the company's strengths and weaknesses

- A thorough understanding of the EC markets in which the company is contemplating entry or expansion

- As accurate a judgement as possible of the impact of the 1992 programme on the company's operations and markets

Certain conclusions can be drawn about how companies should go about formulating their strategies.

Formulation   First, formulation of strategy cannot be left to the marketing people alone. 1992 is not simply a question of whether more people are buying dishwashers and what type is most popular. Nor is it just a matter of the potential for brand marketing across frontiers. 1992 raises far wider issues which, as discussed in the previous chapter, can embrace the future disposition of research and development, manufacturing and distribution activities.

Interpretation   Second, an accurate interpretation of what is happening within the EC is an essential ingredient of successful strategy formulation. Most companies have carried out some form of Euromonitoring activity since Britain first joined the EC in 1973. The work may actually have been done by a trade association, though many large companies possess this capability themselves. Brussels has typically been seen as a source of endless, time-wasting boredom where little of real consequence happens. Within the company, this monitoring will often have been delegated to a single individual.

Organisation   Third, a review of strategy for the single market may have implications for the company's own organisational structure. For example, a multi-product company with an established Continental presence may be organised into a number of financially separate country units, which are competing with each other in terms of performance and the allocation of new investment. Objective analysis may indicate that, to take full advantage of 1992, this structure is in need of a complete overhaul. A radically different structure based on product groups or brands may be appropriate. However, for subjective reasons, senior managers in the country units may be reluctant to recognise this. Only those charged with taking a broad view at senior level may be fully objective about the implications.

High-level direction   All these considerations suggest that a review of European strategy needs to be conducted at the highest level. Moreover, the issues under consideration are of the kind where a suitably qualified non-executive director, perhaps with direct European experience or good political judgement, might well add a useful extra dimension.

Outside advisers   There is, of course, plenty of outside help on which companies can call in order to supplement their own resources. Consultants and outside advisers can fulfil a number of useful roles, including:

- Broad strategic advice on the options for entry or expansion

- Euromonitoring and lobbying as part of 1992 scenario building

- Economic, social and demographic analysis of market opportunities

- Logistical implications of strategic options and preparation of detailed business plans

- Contacts with possible partners
- Help with all aspects of implementing business deals

However, it is probably a mistake to believe that any single set of individuals or organisations is capable of carrying out all these roles with equal effectiveness. Outside advisers complement the company's own deliberations: they are not a substitute for them. The company itself has at all times to be in the driving seat with a firm view of its own strengths and capabilities, giving its advisers a clear brief for their work and keeping abreast of progress at all stages.

These broad judgements are endorsed by many of the case studies in this book. For Christian Salvesen, the initiative in formulating European strategy has come from the top of the company; whatever outside advisers the company may use, there has to be a clear strategic vision from the top. Companies such as De La Rue, London International and Vickers, which operate a large number of different businesses in a highly decentralised way, retain at corporate headquarters a key strategic function which is able to guide the board on the development of the business as a whole. Ransomes Sims & Jefferies set up a board sub-committee specifically to consider the implications of 1992 for all aspects of its business.

Ransomes has also made a feature of seeking to involve its employees wholeheartedly in planning for 1992. Quality meetings have been held throughout the company in which there is expected to be a two-way flow of ideas. One practical result from this process of involvement is that it is stimulating great interest in language learning. While language skills are not a pre-condition for developing a European business strategy, they may turn out to be a great facilitator of its long-term success.

Understanding the market dynamics

An essential ingredient in the process of formulating strategy is a thorough understanding of EC markets.

The single market is an objective: it is not a present-day reality. Each national and regional market within it will continue to have its own distinctive characteristics. The barriers to the completion of a single market consist of far more than can be removed by a programme of political action. Even in a single market, when regulatory barriers are swept away, business opportunities will continue to vary according to factors such as local prosperity, population growth, infrastructure capabilities, consumer preferences and taste, as much as they do in the single UK market today.

The first step in understanding a market is to collate the available statistics about it. In some EC member states and sectors this is easier said than done. This is another point that emerges quite strongly in the case studies. De La Rue found that, in the absence of published official or trade association data, privately owned companies in Spain tend to have little idea of their own market share and tend not to attach much importance to it as long as their own customer base is stable. Ransomes discovered that in France, although figures on imports and exports of grass-cutting machinery are available, the size of the market is extremely difficult to estimate.

Absence of sufficient data may make it worthwhile in some instances for companies to commission their own research. The following checklist sets out some of the basic questions to be asked, although the exact nature of the questions will obviously vary according to the circumstances of the sector.

Checklist of basic questions

1. Market characteristics

- What is the size of each relevant market?
- What is the structure of the relevant markets? Are they dominated by a small number of large players or, at the other extreme, many small businesses?
- What is the trend in each market by volume, by value, etc?
- What changes in consumer attitudes, social patterns, demographic shifts may affect each market?

2. Market position

- What is the company's market share?
- Who are the key competitors?
- To what extent does the company possess Eurobrands – brands with the same name, external packaging and advertising appeal which can be marketed across most or all of the countries of the EC?

3. Market practice

- What methods are presently employed to distribute and market the relevant products in each market?
- How far is marketing practice in each country influenced by regulatory frameworks and cultural attitudes?
- What changes in the availability of marketing tools are in prospect (e.g. satellite television)?

Markets' growth potential

The relevance of the questions on the checklist can be shown by practical illustration. Take the question of market size first. What matters is not just the market's overall size but whether it is growing or, if the overall picture is stable or even declining, whether the company can still identify niches for growth.

Building materials

In building materials, for example, Spain is widely regarded as a rapidly growing market. This reflects in part expectations of rapid economic growth as Spain catches up with its EC neighbours, fostered by the government's liberal attitude to inward investment and the country's relative cheapness as a manufacturing centre in a single market. It also reflects the fact that Spain is hosting two major events in the next five years – the Barcelona Olympics and the Seville World Trade Fair, both of which will require major infrastructure investment.

Steetley, the UK building materials company, saw opportunities in the buoyant Spanish construction sector, and decided to take advantage of them. It has acquired five building materials companies in the Greater Madrid area where it is now thought to account for 20 per cent of the local market in aggregates and 15 per cent of the market in ready mixed concrete. While it still accounts for only 1 per cent of the relevant market in Spain as a whole, Steetley is clearly calculating that rapid economic development will be concentrated on the major urban centres, especially the capital city. It has targeted what it sees as a major growth market.

The Irish CRH group, also a building materials producer, has acquired the Catalan Concrete Group of Barcelona. Both companies see major potential for growth in the expanding Spanish market. CCG is a low-cost producer of concrete with a clear competitive advantage in using power station fly-ash as a cheap additive. It has welcomed the partnership with CRH because for years, as part of a state-owned electricity supply company, it was starved of investment. CRH on the other hand is ready to invest in CCG because it acknowledges that in Spain there would not be a strong market for its own home-produced higher quality products: an interesting example of how differing quality standards are expected to persist in a single market for a long time to come.

Identifying niches

In some markets, growth opportunities may not be as obvious as they are in Spain. Indeed markets may appear saturated and statistics show a more static picture. Here the task is to spot the niches which either existing providers have left untouched or where demographic and social trends may be changing. The provision of mortgage credit is a possible example.

Mortgage credit

Mortgage credit is an area where UK techniques of provision ought to give UK financial institutions a competitive price advantage once 1992 liberalises financial services. The Cecchini report estimated the

47

cost of a mortgage in West Germany, in terms of margin over bank lending rates, as roughly double that in the UK. It is therefore no surprise to find UK banks and building societies probing the potential for entry to these higher priced markets. At first sight, however, they may be greatly discouraged. The West German population is ageing rapidly with implications for future demand for both new housing and mortgages. The existence of a flexible private rented sector, which accounts for more than 60 per cent of the housing stock, obviates the need for young people to jump on the owner-occupation ladder as soon as they can afford it – which contrasts with the UK.

Demographic/social trends

The feasibility of UK entry will depend on whether, against this discouraging picture, there are demographic and social trends which open up new niches. For example, while the West German population may be static and expected to fall, are there growth points involving shifts in population which appear likely to raise housing demand in local situations? Are young people, particularly the better off, as content with renting as they once were? Is the social pattern changing where the elderly live with their families, thus creating the potential for a new market in owner-occupation for retired people?

McCarthy and Stone, the specialist house builder, may have spotted a Continental niche. It has acquired Merlin Immobilier, France's fifth largest company in the second home market. Merlin acts as a developer, spotting and acquiring sites, arranging design and construction, and marketing the finished properties. This acquisition enables McCarthy and Stone to expand the niche market in housing for the retired which it has already exploited in the UK.

Cultural differences

An examination of social and demographic trends opens up the question of cultural differences. Looking again at the mortgage credit example, the question is whether customers on the Continent, if faced with an open choice, prefer the certainties of fixed rate mortgage finance to variable rate mortgages even if it can be shown that, over time, financing by the latter method is much cheaper.

There are many cultural differences which reflect deep-seated national or regional distinctions. For example:

• Cleansing products (such as Ajax) require different chemical formulations for northern and southern European markets. In northern Europe, surfaces tend to be small in area with the detergent powder scattered over the area to be cleaned. In southern Europe, with a much greater preponderance of tiled or wooden flooring, cleansing agents have to be dilutable in water for much more extensive use.

• The pattern of food distribution in West Germany is radically different from that in the UK because of the continuing prevalence of home deliveries in markets such as frozen foods. As a result, freezer centres have never taken off.

- Washing machines are far from homogeneous products within the EC despite the transnational nature of production. The French want their washing machines to load from the top: the British prefer to load from the front. West Germans want high-powered machines that spin most of the dampness out of the clothes: Italians prefer low-powered machines and rely on the sun to do the drying.

- To meet different local tastes, Nescafé markets some twenty different brands of coffee under the same label.

- Consumption of pharmaceuticals varies a great deal as a result of differing health-care practices. In southern Europe, self-medication has traditionally been more prevalent as a result of poorer availability of GP services. But doctors' prescribing practices themselves reflect different attitudes towards the treatment of disease. In West Germany, unlike the UK, low blood-pressure is regarded as a condition requiring extensive medication. In France, doctors regularly prescribe drugs for a heart/digestive condition known as 'spasmophilia', the existence of which doctors in the UK do not even recognise.

Cultural differences will change very slowly. However, they are tending to narrow where people are most mobile and wealthy, and where business is increasingly international.

There is some evidence in our case studies that among the affluent consumer taste is becoming Europeanised. Dawson International sells its Pringle and Ballantyne sweaters in all affluent markets. Emess acquired BrillantLeuchten in West Germany because it identified a growing Europeanisation of taste in decorative lighting and the potential to cross-sell products at the top end of both the West German and UK markets.

The movement towards international business activity is undoubtedly contributing to the Europeanisation of business services in their broadest sense.

The UK computer services firm, CAP, merged with the French firm, Sema Metra, because it believed that its customers increasingly wanted their needs met on an international basis. The new Sema Group is a turnkey supplier of large-scale computer systems in, for example, air traffic control, electronic funds transfer and global securities trading and market-making.

In car hire, interRent (owned by the German company, Volkswagen) and Europcar (owned by the Belgian company, Compagnie Internationale des Wagon-Lits) have set up a joint holding company, presumably in order to pool their respective geographical strengths and serve the market as a single organisation more comprehensively.

There has been considerable international merger activity in the office furniture sector, as companies position themselves to supply the rapidly growing market in flexible office systems. These are built around the new technologies, where most suppliers believe they will increasingly be required to offer international equipment servicing. This is why the UK supplier, Bullough, acquired Atal of France and Roynor of Belgium.

Eurobranding

A key test of the narrowing of cultural differences is the potential for Eurobranding. This was a theme of the so-called 'chocolate wars' and a justification offered for the takeover activities of the Swiss firms, Nestlé and Jacob Suchard. It also featured in the Seagram and Grand Metropolitan takeover battle for Martell and the Pernod Ricard takeover of Irish Distillers.

Eurobranding is one of the prime motivations behind the considerable corporate activity taking place in the advertising field. Agencies are positioning themselves to market Eurobrands through the emergence of satellite television and European publications. They expect companies will want to advertise on an international basis. This is why, for instance, WCRS has taken a stake in the French advertising agency, Belier, and in SGGMD, which brought it the number one spot in media-buying in France. Similarly, WPP has acquired one of the leading advertising groups in the Netherlands, the PPGH Group, in order to fill one of the gaps in its coverage of European centres.

Customising products for local markets

Although many products do not lend themselves to Eurobranding, they can be customised to cater for local market preferences. De La Rue has pursued this strategy by acquiring businesses in specialist niches to which it adds the value of its technological and marketing skills. In West Germany, it has found that an alliance with a local company is the best way for it to win orders for its automatic teller machines and bank-note sorters. West German banks simply would not buy this equipment from a non-German company.

Analysing distribution

Understanding market practice also involves an analysis of distribution arrangements. For existing suppliers, the main question is whether present distribution arrangements will change as a result of 1992. Potential new entrants need to examine whether existing distribution networks tie up the available routes of entry.

Many UK manufacturers traditionally sell their products in Continental markets through dealer networks. Where exclusive arrangements have been agreed, informal market-sharing agreements have often been the result. This is one of the reasons why price differentials have persisted between markets, which has of course enabled manufacturers to earn more profits in higher priced areas than they otherwise would. Most companies are probably content to maintain these arrangements as long as possible, but they are subject to change from two sources. First, the removal of frontier barriers may facilitate far more cross-border parallel trading, putting pressure on margins. Second, competitors may decide present arrangements are unsustainable and make a strategic move which puts their rivals at a disadvantage. For example, if a major competitor withdraws from existing dealership arrangements and decides to set up its own direct sales force, this may force dealers to combine, putting manufacturers who continue to trade through them at a disadvantage in negotiations. Companies should therefore subject their existing distribution arrangements to thorough analysis.

In summary, in framing a European strategy, every business has first to analyse two fundamental issues:

- In its markets, is it fighting the competition on a regional, national, European and/or global battleground?

- What is the main source of competitive advantage in that battle, whether distribution, branding, economies of scale, product range or something else?

5.   Identifying the strategic issues

What is it that drives UK businesses into corporate activity within the European community? In any one case there are probably a number of different motives for a UK company's contemplating such a strategic move. But, for the purposes of understanding business strategies, this chapter draws distinctions between various possible strands of motivation. These are illustrated with real examples at the inevitable risk of ascribing too much weight to one particular facet of any company's thinking.

The following separate strategies can lie behind a move – a desire to:

- Build on strengths and expand geographically rather than diversify into new business areas, as home markets reach saturation point

- Treat the EC as the company's home market in the belief that this is the only way the company can gain the critical mass necessary to fend off global competition

- Seek economies of scale to remain competitive

- Add value to existing businesses, particularly where market structures are fragmented

- Pursue an international marketing strategy

- Get nearer the customer rather than rely on exporting direct

- Expand on the Continent to reduce exposure to risks

- Ensure adequate defences are in place to fend off unwelcome predators

Building on strength

Twenty years ago, diversification was seen as a justifiable way of spreading commercial risk – if one business is depressed, an unrelated business could be thriving, and a group's profits thereby maintained. True conglomeracy was then the sign of a prudent management. Today, except where management teams have built a reputation for extracting value from underperforming businesses, focusing and rationalisation are the watchwords.

Part of this is a product of the recession of the early 1980s. Also, as competition has become ever more intense, senior managers have been forced to concentrate on the areas they know best. Otherwise, in the case of quoted companies, they may face the threat of being taken over by more aggressively managed companies who will seek to realise the value of underperforming assets. It is salutary to realise that factories and high street operations can be worth far more to property developers than to owners of the original business. Senior managers have therefore become schooled in rigorous analysis of the strengths and weaknesses of their business.

The need for a clear focus is evident from the case studies:

- London International has, in the past decade, reduced the number of businesses in which it is actively engaged from thirteen separate activities to five core areas. This has involved withdrawal from areas as varied as paint brushes, electrical accessories and fine china.

- Ransomes has withdrawn from its long-standing presence in the manufacture of fork-lift trucks and farm machinery, businesses which it felt had poor long-term outlooks. It now focuses exclusively on grass-cutting machinery.

- Christian Salvesen has pulled out of its housebuilding and seafoods businesses in order to concentrate resources on what it sees as its key strength – the distribution of temperature-controlled products.

Companies that opt for a focused strategy can find themselves drawn naturally towards expansion abroad, particularly the nearby markets of the Continent. Christian Salvesen started to expand onto the Continent some ten years ago when it thought (incorrectly as it turned out) that the UK market in frozen food distribution was reaching saturation point. Similarly Emess, the lighting specialist, which has enjoyed spectacular growth from its days as a small private company in the early 1980s, decided that it wanted to penetrate the high value-added West German market rather than attempt to push up its 12 to 15 per cent market share in the UK at what it judged to be the expense of margins. Nor has it any desire to turn itself into a mini-conglomerate, which would have been the only other growth option.

Synergistic arguments for expanding into apparently related areas need to be all the more convincing in the case of overseas expansion. This was well illustrated by Vickers' acquisition of a Swiss–German office chair manufacturer. There seemed to be potential for synergy for Vickers' existing office furniture business based in Britain and France. But Swiss–German chair design did not marry successfully with Anglo–French furniture design. The two companies were unable to put together a successful marketing package.

Europe as the home market

Many companies are conscious of intensifying global competition. This may be from other EC-based producers, but the source of the toughest competition is often North America and the Far East. For EC companies, bolstering their position in Europe may be the only strategy available for building up any countervailing strength.

In the commercial grass-cutting market, Ransomes has two main rivals, both American – Toro and Jacobsen, though Japanese producers have also begun to penetrate the market. Unless it can continue to consolidate its position in the European market, it may no longer be feasible for it to remain an independent producer.

The Anglo-French Sema Group has become one of the top ten computer systems companies in the world, and the second largest in Europe. It is well placed as a leading European company in its field to compete with the major US and Japanese companies.

As yet, few UK companies treat Europe as their home market. This is supported by the strong bias towards acquisitions in the USA for most of the 1980s. There are now signs that industries under competitive pressure at home are increasingly seeking alliances in the EC to strengthen their market position against global competitors.

- IMI has bought a 50 per cent stake in R. Woeste, a West German manufacturer of copper plumbing fittings, as well as a 100 per cent stake in the French Raccord Orleanais. Both these companies manufacture products which match those produced by IMI's existing Yorkshire Fittings business, enabling IMI to establish a strong presence in this segment of the market.

- BICC has completed a £90 million deal with the Italian company, Fornara, to acquire its Ceat Cavi cable-manufacturing subsidiary. This will facilitate Anglo-Italian joint ventures in the expanding fields of cable installation and telemetry where BICC faces strong global rivals.

- Coates, the UK printing ink manufacturer, has acquired the Lorilleaux printing ink subsidiary of the French state-owned chemicals group, CDF Chimie SA. This acquisition was justified specifically on the grounds that it would create 'a European company capable of facing up to world competitors', principally BASF of West Germany and Dai Nippon Ink of Japan. Coates' strengths in the UK and Scandinavia are seen as complementing those of Lorilleaux in southern Europe.

Economies of scale

Vertical integration

Economies of scale can be achieved by moves towards either vertical or horizontal integration. A good illustration of vertical integration is provided by the London International case study. LI has gained a competitive edge in photofinishing by achieving high-volume, low-cost production at its processing plants. To maintain and increase that volume it has acquired direct mail companies on the continent that specialise in photoprocessing. Similarly, a major factor underlying Thorn-EMI's successful bid for the French lighting company, Holophane, was the desire to maintain volume in its light-bulb manufacturing plant by gaining control of a significant producer of light fittings. The acquisition bolstered its position as a light-bulb manufacturer against rivals such as Siemens.

Horizontal integration

More typically, economies of scale can be achieved through horizontal mergers, which are the classic form of industrial rationalisation. Though the scope for such activity is considerable in many sectors, cross-border EC rationalisation of this kind is still in its formative stages. There are, however, some interesting early examples.

- In the chemicals industry, ICI and the Italian company Enichem have merged their loss-making PVC manufacturing facilities. This is an instance where the advance approval of the Commission was sought under Article 85(3) of the Treaty of Rome which permits the reduction of competition where the result can be justified on public interest grounds of increased industrial efficiency.

- In the supply of telecommunications equipment, the French

main manufacturer, Alcatel, acquired the European interests of ITT; and the Swedish manufacturer, Ericsson, acquired France's second largest producer, Compagnie Générale de Construction Téléphonique.

- In packaging, the MB Group is trying to sell its packaging interests to the French manufacturing group, Carnaud. A new company has been set up in which MB Group would continue to maintain a minority interest. This new company would be in a strong position to take advantage of the removal of the remaining barriers to a single market in packaging and the harmonisation of technical standards in this area.

Adding value to existing businesses

Technology

Many companies can identify new markets where their technology can be used to enhance products already being sold in the target territory. De La Rue saw this in the West German banking market and has combined its electronic banking systems technology with the products and distribution capacity of Garny, the German company into which it bought. It also found its experience in security printing created synergy with the Dutch lottery ticket printer it acquired.

Management know-how

Adding management know-how is just as beneficial and can be utilised to bring additional value to an acquisition. This is particularly applicable in international markets where localised businesses can benefit considerably from wider management experience. Castrol sees this opportunity frequently and uses it to good effect in its acquisition strategy, often finding that it is a sought-after partner. It recently acquired Consulta, a metal-working oils business in West Germany. Its product had never before been marketed beyond a fifty-mile radius of the plant. Once under Castrol's wing, a much broader marketing effort could be made.

On the Continent, the scope for this type of corporate activity appears considerable. The existence of large numbers of family-owned or controlled companies and the tendency for market structures to be more fragmented, means that the potential gains from the successful application of modern management techniques can be considerable – as long as the ownership, cultural and linguistic barriers to such acquisitions can be overcome.

International marketing

One obvious motive for corporate activity within the EC is the development of international marketing strategies, based on brand names. The principal reasons for such strategies are to:

- Increase market share by popularising a brand name with which the consumer identifies

- Protect and enhance margins by heightening the perceived value of the product against lower cost rivals and new entrants

- Strengthen the manufacturer against any attempt to spread usage of own brands by the retailer

- Streamline manufacturing requirements by inducing consumers to prefer a limited range of products

The previous chapter discussed the potential for Eurobranding. The advent of the single market will create opportunities for greater internationalisation of brands and marketing practices. Nestlé's acquisition of Rowntree showed how highly it valued the relatively local branding displayed by Rowntree in confectionery. Local branding is important for much of the food sector. But there is also a trend towards international branding, especially in alcoholic drinks, as evidenced by the success of Foster's lager from Australia.

Brand building   But how does a company go about this brand-building process in the diverse markets of the EC? Clearly advertising is of great importance, but advertising without a complementary presence on the ground is unlikely to work. One option for a manufacturer like Dawson International would be to set up its own chain of speciality shops throughout the EC either through direct ownership or franchising on the Benetton model. The difficulty here is that, once a manufacturer seeks a direct retail presence at considerable expense, other retail stores will be less keen to stock and give prominence to its goods. Dawson is attempting to square this particular circle by creating a limited number of its own demonstration stores in key European centres, which it hopes will enable it to set trends and market 'apparel concepts' along the lines of the Dunhill model.

Getting nearer the customer

Requirements and perceptions

The branding issue is in one sense a subset of the more general question of how the manufacturer keeps near enough to the customer to influence how the product is packaged and priced and to be sensitive to market opinion and changing consumer preferences. The task is the more complex the wider the market to be served. To achieve its objectives, the manufacturer must either be big enough to control the distribution of its own products or, as long as economies of scale permit, set up its own manufacturing facilities within each main market. Experience throws up examples of both models in the EC.

Local agents

Castrol is an example of a company that has always proceeded by first entering a market after appointing a local agent and later, when the business has grown, acquiring the agent and handling distribution itself. Within the EC it has recently completed this process in all member states, most recently Spain and Greece, with the exception that in Portugal distribution is handled by a joint venture between Castrol and the formerly independent agent.

At this stage, evidence of others following this model is limited. IMI has, however, recently acquired the Belgian distributor of the pneumatic products manufactured by its Norgren and Martonair subsidiaries. Other companies may be contemplating this type of move, particularly where they are big enough and have exclusive dealership arrangements.

Manufacturing plants

Setting up satellite manufacturing plants near local markets is a logical step when domestic capacity is fully utilised or manufacturing economies of scale are not large. For instance, most pharmaceutical companies have served their markets from localised plant even at some cost in foregone economies of scale. An interesting case is the specialist chemicals company, Marlborough Technical Management. It has come under pressure from its Continental customers, which has led it to set up facilities near them. This may reflect either a feeling that proximity guarantees reliability of supply, or a more general concern that customers prefer local suppliers.

Reducing exposure to risks

One clear motive for corporate activity is to attempt to reduce exposure to risks. Such risks might include:

- Interrupted production due to supplier problems or industrial action

- Over-exposure to the fortunes of a single customer

- Currency risks

Industrial relations

Fears of interrupted production used to be a major factor in framing UK business strategies. But conditions have radically changed in the last decade. One of the interesting footnotes to this study is that UK companies do not cite industrial relations as a reason for making a move into Europe.

Many UK companies are, however, still over-exposed to the fortunes of a single customer or a small group. Many motor component firms are still linked to the viability of the Rover Group. In connection with this, one interesting Continental acquisition was that by Laird of CPIO, a Renault supplier which Laird acquired from Renault itself. This reduced the risk of exposure for both parties – Renault weakening the power of its unions by disposing of a supplier to another company, Laird widening its customer base.

Currency exposure

Currency exposure is another risk factor. Companies with high exposure to the dollar are now looking to Continental acquisitions in order to balance the position. This was given as one reason for the WCRS acquisition of stakes in the Paris advertising agency, Belier, and SGGMD, the French media buyer. It was also cited as a contributory factor in the British Aerospace purchase of the Dutch civil engineering company, Ballast Nedam.

Defence against takeovers

UK quoted companies seen as soft targets

Following the Rowntree takeover by Nestlé, many quoted UK companies came to realise that the creation of the more competitive environment brought about by the single market could lead to more aggressive takeovers by foreign companies of UK targets. In fact, it has always been possible for UK-quoted companies without significant 'blocking' shareholdings to be taken over against their management's will. Moreover, the UK equity markets are far more open than any other in the EC. More information is available and the markets are far more liquid. Incumbent UK management has much less ability to frustrate predators than most of their Continental counterparts. There is certainly no room for complacency.

Hostile takeovers	However, hostile takeovers by EC companies are extremely rare. That is not to say that UK-quoted companies should drop their guard against possible predators from across the Channel, but a greater threat could be from non-EC companies seeking to promote or protect their position in the single market. A Directive has been drafted covering the conduct of takeovers in the Community. This is still in the consultative phase, and will in any event take several years to implement. Even when it arrives, it will in itself do nothing to change the structure of overseas markets and the fundamental differences in terms of the openness and shareholding structures of the companies whose shares are traded in those markets. This is dealt with in more detail later.

Most takeovers are made on an agreed basis and this will continue to be the case. However, as UK-quoted companies are softer targets for hostile activity, it is important to ensure that appropriate defences are in place. Each company needs to agree sensible defence strategies with its financial advisers.

Regardless of the nationality of the anticipated predator, strategies should include:

- Maintaining and improving profits

- Maintaining good public and investor relations, to include regular briefings for analysts, other commentators and major shareholders

- Constant monitoring of the share register, particularly nominee shareholdings

- Ensuring adequate access to political and other relevant authorities

- Maintaining good relations with customers and suppliers

- Monitoring market share in key product areas: this may be relevant in the event of a competition reference

- Setting up a board committee with full authority to co-ordinate a defence, and briefing all necessary advisers

- Reviewing possible predators and 'white knights' (friendly bidders)

- Ensuring that management accounts, budgets and valuations are regularly updated

- Considering other defensive options, such as management buyout, acquisitions and disposals

This all pre-supposes that the management is actively managing the business to enhance earnings per share, dividends and dividend cover and thereby share price. Constant review of operations is necessary to identify areas of weakness and continuing areas of strength.

The essence of these strategies is to ensure, as far as possible, that the company is ready to react effectively and quickly to any hostile approach. Time is very short in a bid situation.

Even the best-prepared defence can sometimes face overwhelming odds. In the Rowntree case, Nestlé's chequebook was so large and its concern about possible earnings dilution from an expensive acquisition so small, that there was relatively little the management could do except attempt to raise the price (which was successfully achieved) and obtain a monopolies referral (which was not).

Defence against an overseas predator does, however, involve additional considerations not relevant in a domestic takeover battle in the UK:

- Information on EC companies is generally less accessible than in the UK, making it harder to identify vulnerabilities. The beneficial ownership of shares held by overseas nominees may be difficult to establish and it may not be possible to take fully effective action where requests for disclosure are not complied with. Accordingly, consideration should be given to including disenfranchisement provisions in the Articles of Association.

- Continental companies tend to be less sensitive to their own shareholders' attitudes and therefore less susceptible to criticism for paying an excessive price.

- There is more likely to be an effect on trade between member states resulting from a cross-border takeover in the EC, than a domestic takeover in the UK. EC competition policy – and in particular the draft Merger Control Regulation – could well come into play for any takeover involving a large company.

- Political issues, especially in the employment area, may be significant. A remote employer could be seen as less sensitive to criticism of its local employment practices. The presence of material military or other sensitive contracts could also be significant.

- The issue of lack of reciprocity – unequal circumstances for the bidder and the target – may be relevant in certain circumstances. While the UK competition authorities do not specifically take this into account, UK investors and politicians could be influenced by this issue.

There is no doubt that defensive moves against takeover threats have featured large in the motivations for some corporate activity in advance of 1992.

The share swap between Pearson, the UK conglomerate which owns the *Financial Times*, and the Dutch publisher, Elsevier, reflected the complementary nature of certain of their ventures. But there were undoubtedly additional attractions to Pearson – it counteracted News International's unwelcome stake and established a major friendly shareholder.

Again, the basis for the UK insurer, Sun Life, seeking alliances in the EC is logical, given the problem of gaining direct entry to the Continental insurance market from a standing start. But Sun Life, like other companies in the sector, has had unwelcome shareholders for some time and the friendly shareholding taken by UAP, the French insurer, was probably, to some extent, defensive in purpose.

Many different strategies can therefore lie behind a company's approach to the single market. But having developed a clear view of its strategic objectives, a company must then choose between a whole variety of different routes for expansion.

6. Routes for expansion

The single market means that businesses will have easier access to over 320 million end-customers. Businesses will therefore have greater opportunity to expand into other member states, taking advantage of the removal or simplification of the barriers which have hitherto made this difficult.

The first result of economic integration is of course an increase in trade. As a result of 1992, the two-way flow of exports and imports will undoubtedly increase. This chapter, however, looks beyond the trade potential of 1992.

Many of the attendant issues that arise in expanding exports in terms of marketing, distribution and branding have already been discussed. But the need for UK companies to develop a greater physical presence on the Continent is becoming increasingly apparent. The options open to them include:

- Greenfield development

- Trading relationships

- Minority stakes and strategic alliances

- Joint ventures

- Acquisitions and mergers

Greenfield development

High risks

This differs from simple organic growth by export in that the company establishes a new operation in an overseas market. This can be a high risk strategy. Start-up costs can be considerable. Effective local management has to be found and carefully monitored. Infrastructure has to be set up – sales and other staff, warehousing, production facilities, communications, local banking arrangements, property, etc. Materials supply has to be arranged and local regulations need to be complied with. Distribution arrangements have to be put in place.

Analysing the market

The reaction of local competitors needs to be assessed, as well as the acceptability of the company's products.

The starting point must be to identify whether there is a market opportunity. Analysis of the target market may, however, lead to the view that greenfield development is not feasible because of the strength of local competition. There may not be room for a major new participant in the market, as Grampian's sports division recognised in West Germany, where Adidas and Puma dominate the market.

Familiarity with the workings of the relevant market is particularly important. CAP, before its merger with Sema Metra of France, had established greenfield operations in the Netherlands, Singapore and the USA, but found that organic growth in these businesses was slow and difficult because of their unfamiliarity with the markets being serviced.

The prospects for greenfield entry are most promising where existing export sales into the target territory indicate that there is sufficient demand to justify local production. The presence of existing infrastructure for another of the company's activities may assist a new operation. Another possibility is where a key materials supplier is located in the target territory, with clear advantages for setting up a new production facility nearby. Alternatively, it may be possible to follow an existing customer into a new territory, as Christian Salvesen has done. In any sector where a company possesses major financial muscle, the greenfield strategy may be feasible as long as the company is capable and willing to make the necessary investment and perhaps take losses in the early years.

Trading relationships

Entering into a trading relationship is often seen as an alternative to investing in, or buying, someone else's business. And so it may be. However, such a relationship can be a very useful adjunct either before or at the same time as a direct investment.

Trading relationships can be the most satisfactory way of entering new markets, especially for companies without surplus management resources, who do not want to commit the necessary capital to invest in building their own business in the market, and who do not have the treasury skills to manage the exchange and interest rate implications of owning overseas assets and repatriating foreign earnings.

Moreover, in some markets, it can be very difficult to find owners willing to sell an interest in their business. They need to feel something more is to be gained in a tangible and visible form. Their confidence has to be won and direct knowledge of each other's business obtained before an acquisition or more formalised relationship can be contemplated.

A distributorship agreement can therefore be an important first step. Such an arrangement was used, for example, by Leyland Trucks and Daf for distribution of Leyland trucks on the Continent. The result for Leyland Trucks was an eventual merger, creating a major multinational Community business.

Trading relationships are indeed commonplace throughout the EC, especially for producers of sophisticated products where product development is both costly and lengthy. Most motor vehicle manufacturers share technology and facilities. Service companies – merchant banks among them – see great benefit from collaboration, especially where business straddles frontiers. There are no prizes for companies who insist on going it alone and fail; and no shame in recognising limitations and finding like-minded partners.

Strategic links and minority equity stakes

Benefits from participation

The acquisition of a minority equity interest is a very different approach. It differs from acquisitions in that control remains with the vendors. But an agreed minority equity interest will also allow the company to share in the benefits which its participation in the target business will bring: for example, in gaining direct experience of the new market and acting as a useful back-up to a trading relationship, which perhaps provides for mutual distribution in each other's markets or technology-sharing arrangements. It will also probably give the UK company some say on the target company's board, without the burden of hands-on management, and may block a sale to a third party competitor.

Other reasons for taking only a minority interest include:

- Up-front cost limitation
- To incentivise management
- To strengthen defences against the threat of takeover
- The easiest way in to attractive businesses
- To overcome political objections

. 67

A minority stake, because it does not bring control, generally costs less than a direct proportion of the value of the whole – 30 per cent is worth less than half of 60 per cent. By the same token, because there are different degrees of control, smaller minorities come cheaper in relative terms than larger ones: especially either side of the 25 per cent level, which typically triggers various blocking mechanisms.

One of the reasons for making an acquisition, rather than trying to sell the company's wares into the target territory, could well be the presence of entry barriers, such as high setting-up costs or local brand loyalty. If, however, a market is particularly difficult to enter, and if its attractions are enough to interest the UK company, it is probably also one in which potential vendors will be less willing to sell. On the other hand, access to the UK company's skills and technology, not to mention capital, could offer strong incentives for the vendors to agree to offer the UK company a minority stake. The management of the West German lighting company, BrillantLeuchten, originally refused to let Emess buy the company outright. They limited Emess to a stake of less than 25 per cent in the first instance, only agreeing to sell a controlling interest a year later when Emess's good intentions towards the West German company had been demonstrated.

Local political objections

Political objections were a key factor in respect of the limitation of AT&T's stake in Olivetti to 25 per cent. When this deal was announced, it won widespread support in Italy on the grounds that it would greatly improve Olivetti's chances of winning business in the US market (which it has). In contrast, when in spring 1988 Carlo de Benedetti claimed that AT&T wished to increase its stake to a controlling figure, this caused local political uproar.

The same lesson emerges in a lower profile way in the Pearson bid for the French financial paper, *Les Échos*. Despite strong support for the bid from proprietor and management, political factors led the French government to insist that Pearson reduce its bid for 100 per cent to one for only a majority stake.

Management incentives

A problem with outright acquisitions is that it is always difficult to motivate a management team that has just received large amounts of money for its business. One way around this is to replace them. A less drastic course, which may particularly suit people businesses, is to take only a minority stake, giving the existing team every incentive to continue to make profits. This is the strategy many in the advertising and public relations worlds are pursuing in their efforts to build agencies with worldwide links and capabilities, though often the balance of the equity will be acquired on a pre-determined earn-out basis.

In Chapter 5, examples were given of recent EC deals involving minority stakes, in which at least one important factor was their advantage as a defensive move against takeover. While each of these deals has its own commercial logic, the motive of acquiring a friendly minority shareholder must have been present. As regards minority equity stakes in general, from the target company's viewpoint there is a welcome inflow of funds, either to the shareholders or to the company itself, and an international dimension is achieved with minimal effort. For most potential acquirers, there is the advantage that at some future date an existing shareholder is well placed to win more equity should this become available. It may also be possible to negotiate a pre-emption right over more of the equity, or perhaps just an option, thus adding a further attraction to the acquisition of a minority interest.

Disadvantages

Many companies are sceptical about minority equity stakes and so-called strategic alliances. De La Rue, for example, is disinclined to take minority stakes in other companies, even with pre-emption rights over the remaining equity. It feels that the potential arguments about future development of the business and how to deal with profits make such arrangements unattractive. It would prefer a clearer arrangement involving, say, a royalty on sales of products using De La Rue's technology. However, De La Rue did take a 49 per cent minority stake in the West German manufacturer, Garny, when it realised there was no other practical way into the crucial German market.

Minority stakes have always been more favoured on the Continent than in the UK. One reason may be the presence, in quoted UK companies, of like-minded institutional shareholders who typically hold the majority of the equity. A minority industrial shareholder may well, therefore, face concerted opposition to its commercial interests. On the Continent, however, institutional shareholding is far less organised, and a substantial minority shareholder can reasonably expect to have much greater influence over the affairs of a company.

Concert parties

Moreover, 'concert party' type arrangements between shareholders are a feature of Continental quoted company life in circumstances which would not be possible in the UK. De Benedetti, for example, uses just this kind of mechanism for controlling his empire, and indeed used it in his ambitious bid for Belgium's largest company, Société Générale de Belgique. It will be interesting to see whether UK companies become more prepared to follow this route in their Continental expansion, if for no other reason than the unavailability of a controlling interest.

Joint ventures

Joint ventures, unlike share swaps or minority stakes, involve two or more partners each vesting part of its assets in some form of jointly run operation. Most business executives are cautious about joint ventures because of problems over ultimate control and because divergent development of the partners' own businesses may cause conflict. However, where they are based on very particular strategic goals and special situations, they can be very successful.

- Where the alternative to a joint venture is cut-throat competition
- Where technological co-operation is required
- Where project development costs are otherwise prohibitive

Solvay of Belgium and Laporte of the UK have had good experience with their Interox collaboration, which produces a large proportion of the world's peroxide. This is backed up by Solvay's substantial shareholding in Laporte.

Similarly, the ICI–Enichem joint venture, called the European Vinyls Corporation, is a means of rationalising an industry suffering from chronic over-capacity. The joint venture already had a significant market share in its core business when it was set up in December 1987. It subsequently acquired three European PVC businesses and aims to develop its plastics business further.

Development costs in the airliner business are huge. Airbus, the four-nation European consortium, is the only serious competitor to Boeing, apart from McDonnell Douglas. The Airbus consortium has been able to compete only by pooling the massive development costs and benefiting from considerable government subsidies.

The joint venture to produce videos between Thorn–EMI, Telefunken and Japan's JVC is an example of how, by cooperating with one of the two leading Japanese suppliers, European companies were able to salvage some profitable business from what might otherwise have been an expensive disaster for them. At the time videos were launched on the market, there was great technological uncertainty as to which system would eventually dominate the business. By entering into an arrangement with JVC, rather than taking the risk of producing their own models, these European companies were able to benefit as manufacturers, while giving an impetus to the JVC standard.

Management difficulties

Joint ventures are often driven by the need to match two sets of complementary business strengths. It is the management of the joint venture which often presents the greatest problems. Very often, in a 50–50 joint venture, there will be joint or alternating chairmen and equal participation on the board, joint auditors, joint legal and financial advisers, etc. The partners in joint ventures can easily end up managing the business twice, or at least paying excessively for the costs of management.

Cross-border joint ventures bring additional problems. Communication between the two sides may require advanced language skills. Different accounting practices will have to be reconciled, and appropriate consolidations made in parent company accounts. The official location of the joint venture may be critical for tax purposes. Joint ventures should not, therefore, be undertaken lightly.

Acquisitions and mergers

The options other than acquisitions for entering new overseas markets have their problems, but they are nevertheless historically more common on the Continent. One reason is that ownership and management tend to be more closely related than in the UK. Floating a family company on the stock market is a normal goal for a successful business in the UK. But on the Continent, the stock markets are less developed and attitudes to selling off all or part of the equity in a business are therefore different.

In an outright acquisition, the acquiring company has complete control. It is in many ways the simplest option to bring to fruition but the hardest to manage thereafter. In fact, it can reasonably be looked on as a shortcut to greenfield development. The approach to acquisitions is dealt with fully in succeeding chapters.

As an alternative to buying the target business as a going concern, there is the option of buying some or all of its assets. This is a very different concept and probably requires the acquiring company to have existing local management competence in the target territory. It may be buying a factory, a brand name, or a technology and can be cheaper where company values exceed those of the underlying assets. The key difference is that it does not involve investing in an on-going business.

Mergers can be distinguished from acquisitions and joint ventures mainly by the scale of the parties' commitment to the venture. They are often achieved by creating a new top company, and injecting all the business and assets of the parties into this. Alternatively, one company can offer its equity to the shareholders of the other company.

A good example of a cross-border European merger is Sema Group – the combination of CAP, the UK computer software business, and its French counterpart, Sema Metra. The story is told fully in the case study (p. 80), but it is interesting to note that the senior management on both sides considered all options short of merger. However, they came to the conclusion that merger was the only practical option.

Defensive mergers   Mergers may be born out of defensive motives, where both companies see themselves as vulnerable either to competition or to

71

takeover. They may, on the other hand, be the logical progression from long-standing links, technology transfer agreements, and the like. Or they may derive, as in the Sema Group, from customer needs, where a greater range of service is required, or simply greater size to handle larger contracts.

There are, therefore, a number of different routes by which companies can seek to expand on the Continent. Clearly the route chosen must reflect the best available compromise between the strategic objectives discussed in the previous chapter, and practical constraints.

A company seeking to realise manufacturing economies of scale will not be interested in greenfield developments. Equally, a company concerned about possible predators may be anxious to obtain a friendly minority shareholder rather than weaken its financial position by expensive acquisition or costly greenfield development. Trading relationships may be attractive either to companies seeking distribution outlets as part of a Eurobranding strategy, or wanting to customise their products to cultural differences between national markets.

Strategic objectives will therefore suggest some routes rather than others. The choice between the available options should then depend on a realistic assessment of the relevant constraints, particularly:

- The limitations of the company's managerial capacities

- The relative initial costs of any option

- The company's financial strength to withstand losses or inject additional capital in the early years.

CASE STUDY

De La Rue
Accessing markets through acquisition

*Report of an interview with Peter Shires, Commercial
Development Manager*

De La Rue is best known as the printer of bank notes and passports. In
fact it manages a wide diversity of businesses, all of which are related
to security or printing with a heavy emphasis on technology. For
example, the core business of printing bank notes has led to a special-
isation in the technology of payments systems, in particular the software that drives them: 'the innards of automatic billing machines and
bank note sorters', as Peter Shires describes them; De La Rue's skills
in printing high-security items have extended into the management of
security and identity systems; while its Crosfield subsidiary, which
now accounts for 40 per cent of revenues, is a market leader in certain
types of pre-press printing technology. Although the markets in
which the company operates are various, and its structure is highly
decentralised with a small head office, there is a certain homogeneity
about its identity: it is software driven and high technology based.

   Although De La Rue has traditionally been a big exporter, in recent
years it has pursued a strategy of building up its operations in the rest
of Europe. These now account for 20 per cent of the company's total
turnover. As Peter Shires puts it, 'Europe is our home market. We
have pursued a strategy of acquisitions and joint ventures, identifying
businesses where we can add value both through our technical expertise and the strength of our marketing position.'

   De La Rue's range of European experience is therefore considerable. It has adopted three methods to penetrate the Continental
market – direct distribution of UK products, joint ventures and
acquisition. These varieties of approach can be illustrated by recent
activities.

   The Crosfield printing technology business has relied solely on
setting up its own distribution subsidiaries. However, in West Germany
the joint venture route was chosen where De La Rue took a stake in

Garny, a West German manufacturer of payment systems equipment. De La Rue was anxious to build a strong position in the West German bank market in this area. Greenfield entry made little sense – first because there was not room in the market for a major new player and secondly because West German banks have always exhibited a strong preference for giving business to West German companies.

The joint venture with Garny enabled De La Rue to add its own considerable technical strengths and product range to that of the existing company while customising the product for the needs of the West German market. Garny for its part had considerable marketing strengths which worked to De La Rue's advantage. De La Rue insisted however, despite accepting the status of minority partner, on the appointment of a British managing director. The De La Rue–Garny joint venture now has a market share ranging from 5 per cent to 40 per cent in the relevant markets.

In the Netherlands, De La Rue purchased ILS – a lottery ticket printer. The ILS business was a logical fit with De La Rue's existing activities in security printing. In order to defer the owner's tax liability, the consideration was satisfied by the issue of new De La Rue shares – unusual in so far as most European vendors typically prefer cash.

As an example of a recent Continental acquisition, Peter Shires described in detail De La Rue's purchase of the Spanish security printing firm, Lerchundi. De La Rue decided to acquire a security printing firm in Spain, as a means of gaining access to the local market.

It was not familiar with the market, so it first commissioned its own survey. This identified various possibilities, of which Lerchundi – a family-owned firm with plants in Bilbao, Madrid and Barcelona – seemed the best prospect. Ownership of Lerchundi was divided into two family groupings. As it happened, one of the shareholding groups took the initiative in approaching De La Rue. This was because De La Rue had adopted a totally open approach in conducting its market survey in the belief that this was the only way companies in southern Europe would be forthcoming. Such openness is important, De La Rue believes, since companies may fear that the source of the investigation is the tax authorities.

De La Rue then approached the other half of the family. It used the good offices of a prominent local contact who is a regional director of De La Rue and a director of the Bank of Bilbao. His role in the successful completion of the acquisition was central and critical.

It quickly emerged that the family were keen to sell, but had no idea how to value the company. Nor were their bank advisers much better placed. The accounts had to be examined fully and the principles of valuation patiently explained. Much effort went into winning the owners' confidence that De La Rue was willing to pay a fair price.

Another difficult area in the negotiations was De La Rue's insistence that all members of the Lerchundi family give up any management connection with the company. This was because family members populated all levels of management and De La Rue took the view early in the discussions that they would all have to leave the company if effective management was to be instituted. This was a judgement based on the particular circumstances of the company in question, not a general rule De La Rue applies. Another crucial aspect of the deal was to win the confidence of the Basque trade unions. Prior to the deal, De La Rue gave assurances about the collective agreements that would apply after the purchase.

The success of De La Rue's approach became evident at a late stage in the negotiations. A major hiccup occurred after several months when a major fire destroyed most of the Bilbao plant. However, by this stage the family's confidence in De La Rue was such that they accepted that there had to be a significant adjustment in the price paid and that De La Rue should take 100 per cent, not a 70 per cent stake as originally planned. The deal went through.

Another encouraging feature of the story was that in spite of the disruption to production the fire caused, and the need to sub-contract work to competing suppliers, customers remained remarkably loyal. De La Rue put a UK management team into the plant with the aim of building up the local management. They felt able to withdraw it eighteen months after the purchase.

As a general rule De La Rue has a policy of not launching hostile bids. This is largely because of their strong preference for keeping the existing management in place if at all possible. To maintain incentives, it has found earn-out arrangements are a useful tool.

Peter Shires stresses five particular points arising from his experience:

- It is essential to understand the markets in which potential acquisitions are operating. Data is scarce and family-owned companies operating in a stable environment rarely think in terms of growth potential.

- A judgement must be made early about the quality of the local management. Keep them if possible, and be clear in explaining where they will fit into the new structure. If they are not required, act clearly and decisively.

- Strong local contacts are crucial in establishing good relations with vendors. De La Rue sustains a network of such consultants throughout the EC.

- Speed is essential in dealing with small companies: they fear a big organisation will never make up its mind.

- Minority stakes are not generally a good idea, even with rights of first refusal on future share purchases. Arguments about future profits can be very difficult. Rather than take a minority it is often more satisfactory to agree a royalty on sales, as De La Rue has done where it is seeking to graft some of its own product range onto an existing operation.

Vickers
Moving into Europe

Report of an interview with Bill Foreman,
Commercial Director

Over the last twelve years Vickers has undergone large-scale restructuring. A change of emphasis was in the first place forced on the company from the outside with the nationalisation of Vickers' shipbuilding and aircraft interests by the last Labour government in 1977. In 1980 Vickers acquired the Rolls-Royce and Bentley car businesses, which is now the group's largest division and accounts for a quarter of the group turnover.

There are four other main businesses within the group:

- The Vickers defence division, which is the only UK supplier of battletanks.

- Howson-Algraphy, which produces printing plates and is the third largest manufacturer in the world.

- The marine engineering division, which manufactures components such as propellers, steering gears, thrusters and water-jet propulsion units.

- The medical business, which specialises in neo-natal intensive care products and monitoring equipment. A strategic decision on Vickers' part to expand this business led to the acquisition of the Danish manufacturer, S & W Medico Teknik in April 1988.

As Bill Foreman readily acknowledges, the main focus of Vickers' activities in the last decade has been more on the USA than on the Continent.

Seventy-five per cent of Rolls-Royce and Bentley cars were sold in either the UK or the USA, with about 12 per cent going to Continental Europe. The division has a strong network of distributors on the Continent, having its own sales office based on Switzerland, and although the percentage of output to Continental Europe is unlikely to change materially in the foreseeable future, a steady increase in volume is expected.

The defence business has traditionally been nationally based, but Bill Foreman does note that governments are progressively demanding the best product at the most competitive price and this may lead to a situation where national purchasing may not be supplied either in part or in whole by the indigenous manufacturers. In response to this changing scene he expects a strengthening of European joint ventures and other commercial associations. Vickers already has a collaborative arrangement with a major West German supplier which may become more significant in the years ahead.

Howson-Algraphy's production is centred in Leeds, which accounts for 80 per cent of its output, with smaller factories in the Netherlands and Spain. Its distribution chain throughout Europe and the rest of the world is strong, with a mix of both sales subsidiaries and independent dealers. Vickers is not anticipating any major change in these arrangements as a result of 1992.

Vickers does see scope for rationalisation in the marine engineering business, as there is excess capacity in Europe where increasingly strong competition from the Far East is being faced.

In the medical division, Vickers has made a conscious effort to establish a strong Continental presence. This lay behind the decision to acquire the Danish firm S & W Medico Teknik. Vickers was attracted to S & W for two main reasons:

- It had high-quality products complementary to Vickers' own, which would enable economies of scale in distribution and marketing to be realised.

- It also had a presence in West Germany, which with the division's existing network elsewhere in Europe would enable the division's entire medical product range to be directly marketed throughout most of the EC member states.

Vickers knew of S & W through its own management in the medical equipment business. A distribution link already existed as a result of a US acquisition Vickers had made two years earlier. S & W was effectively owned and managed by one individual who had a very high reputation in Denmark. Now, approaching retirement, he was thought to be looking for a good home for the business he had successfully developed.

The negotiations to acquire S & W were protracted, with the initial discussions revealing a wide gap on price. After a series of meetings this gap was ultimately bridged, but owing to other circumstances, the parties were unable to reach final agreement and discussions were terminated.

Because of the mutual feeling that such a deal would be in the best interests of S & W, the owner and Vickers, negotiations were resumed after a lapse of a few months and thereafter the transaction was quickly concluded.

As with all its acquisitions, Vickers handled the S & W transaction in-house, with the assistance of local lawyers. The acquisition team was headed by Bill Foreman with two executives from the medical division and two specialists in law and financial appraisal from headquarters.

Vickers will continue to search for attractive acquisition and collaborative opportunities in Europe but because of the rather specialised nature of certain of its core businesses, the most likely avenues will be in medical and marine engineering.

Sema Group
Merging to remain competitive

Report of an interview with John Chisholm,
UK Managing Director

The merger of the British computer services company CAP and its French counterpart Sema Metra is a rare instance of a conscious attempt to create a pan-European world player in an advanced technological, high value-added field. CAP and Sema Metra both have strengths in the turnkey supply of large-scale computer systems – for example, for air-traffic control, industrial automation, electronic funds transfer, global securities trading and market-making. Their merger puts the company among the top ten computer systems companies in the world and makes it one of the largest in Europe.

John Chisholm sees the merger as a logical consequence of 'the steadily increasing minimum size necessary to be competitive'. Scale has a number of aspects. The industry enjoyed rapid growth in the last two decades with the size of the market growing by an estimated 20 per cent a year consistently throughout the 1980s. As the market has expanded, so has the size of the contracts for which CAP has had to bid. 'The latest contract we obtained in the defence field involved some 240 man-years of work.' As average contract-size has risen, so has the risk associated with any one contract unless it can be spread over a much bigger operation.

At the same time, computer systems organisations are beginning to compete with the big electronics manufacturers. For example, the new Sema Group has recently won contracts in competition with GEC for rail signalling and with Ferranti for defence equipment. But to win these contracts, it had to be big.

Size enables computer systems companies to achieve economies of scale in training staff, the industry's key resource: these would not otherwise be achievable. In addition 'in this area big clients tend to want big companies to work for them. In our field they want to feel we can look at their problems on a pan-European basis.'

All these considerations led CAP in the mid-1980s, particularly after it went public in 1985, to develop and implement an acquisitions strategy. John Chisholm explains it in these terms: 'We are a rapidly maturing industry. Although there were still thousands of new starts last year, there is consolidation worldwide at the top. Last year there were some 450 acquisitions involving computer services companies.'

CAP has made some half-a-dozen acquisitions in the last few years but in 1987 85 per cent of its revenues were still UK-based. Although it had established small greenfield operations in the Netherlands, the USA and Singapore, organic growth proved very slow and difficult in markets it did not know well. 'The logical place for us to think of a strategic move was on the Continent, particularly France.' Apart from the UK, the industry is only well developed in France. The other major competitors are mostly based in the USA.

In selecting a French company for some form of strategic alliance, there were really only two choices – Sema Metra, its eventual partner, and CGS. In the mid-1970s CGS bought out a venture which CAP had established in France, and there had been no further connection with the company. Although CGS is the bigger of the French companies, CAP saw Sema Metra as a better fit.

CAP and Sema Metra together examined a wide variety of mechanisms by which a relationship might be cemented – consortia, a technology transfer agreement, minority cross-shareholdings – but none of these seemed very attractive. CAP's experience of consortia and technology transfer agreements was that they never really worked. Minority cross-shareholdings had the problem of taxation on two-way dividend flows. 'Eventually both sides came to the conclusion that the only real option was full merger. It took us a full year to negotiate.' Ultimately it was agreed that the most tax-effective mechanism was for CAP to offer its equity from Sema Metra. John Chisholm thinks there are two main reasons why the merger went through. 'In the first place there were benefits for all to see, and no one lost out. There was little geographical overlap in the two companies' markets. There was no need for urgent rationalisation.' More positively, the merger opened up immediate new business opportunities. For example, in the UK CAP has developed the software for the Cellnet telephone system. With the forthcoming adoption of a European standard for cellular telephones, the new Sema Group is now in a strong position to sell its product to the French PTT, with whom Sema Metra has historically an extremely close relationship. 'Without the merger, selling to the French would have been much more difficult.'

The second main reason why the merger went through was the sympathy of the authorities in both countries. In the UK CAP has a heavy involvement with the Ministry of Defence. Defence-related work generates about 30 per cent of turnover. Sema Metra is in a similar position in France. The Ministry of Defence required assurances that following the merger defence work would be 'ring fenced'. Similarly the French Defence Ministry was eventually persuaded that the merged company should retain its status as an authorised French defence contractor. John Chisholm believes that 'a few years earlier the defence arguments would have killed the proposed merger stone dead. We would never have made progress without a change of attitude and the authorities' tacit approval.'

The political dimension was even more important in France because the formerly state-owned bank, Paribas, held a majority stake in Sema Metra. But Paribas still retained extremely close links with French politicians and, as a result of these, any potential opposition there might have been to the merger was satisfied.

What were the key issues in negotiating a successful merger? A point of delicate sensitivity was where the new company should be headquartered, or rather, where the holding company should be registered. Both CAP and Sema Metra wanted the merged company to be perceived as European, not Anglo-French. For that reason the Netherlands had been seriously considered for the holding company's registered office. But at the end of the day, all accepted that for tax reasons it was much better to make the UK the headquarters in both fact and name. There is now a Spaniard on the board, which demonstrates a pan-European commitment.

Another area of difference is the board structure of the new company. The merged company ended up with far more non-executive directors than we are accustomed to in the UK. 'In fact the non-executives are in a small majority, but we also put the Sema Metra executives on the board for the first time.'

The company has ended up with, in John Chisholm's words, 'perhaps too top-heavy a committee structure'. Meetings have been longer and larger. 'There's been a need for a lot of talking because there's less of an accumulated common pool of knowledge.' He regards this as a transitional stage. Once people get to know each other better, it is likely that the structure can be streamlined.

Executive responsibilities have been carefully split between the top management. Functional roles have been established for the whole of the merged company in key areas such as R&D, a step regarded as essential to achieve economies of scale. Multinational 'task groups' have been set up to develop marketing strategies for business areas when there is a strong multinational presence, such as financial services.

One awkwardness for the new company is the stake the French company, CGS, has chosen to build up in it. John Chisholm dismisses the possibility of takeover because of the security presented by the Paribas holding. But he regrets the extent to which, as CGS has built up its stake, less than 25 per cent of the company is now UK-owned. The Sema Group retains a quote on the Paris Bourse. While shareholders are sometimes more difficult to identify in France, the need to keep both UK and French investors well informed on group activity and prospects is regarded as a vital management task.

John Chisholm's key messages for businessmen contemplating cross-border mergers can be summarised as follows:

- 'Remember the need for endless talk.'

- 'There will in the short term be added cost and complexity: duplication will take time to eliminate.'

- 'A commitment to language learning is essential; even though the official language of the group is English, on important matters people have to be able to communicate in their native language.'

Ransomes Sims & Jefferies
Be European for independence and growth

*Report of an interview with Sandy Cameron, Executive
Director and Company Secretary*

Ransomes celebrates its 200th anniversary in 1989 and until compara-
tively recently its main business was in farm machinery, with both
fork-lift trucks and grass-cutting machinery something of Cinder-
ellas, particularly in export terms. In the early 1980s Ransomes was
forced to restructure its business drastically. It first sold its fork-lift
trucks operations. However, the general depression in the agricultural
machinery business and poor long-term outlook eventually led
Ransomes to dispose of this business to Electrolux in November 1987.
The focus of Ransomes' business is now exclusively grass-cutting. In
the mid-1980s, it added to its traditional strengths in the commercial
grass-cutting market by the acquisition of Mountfield, a Maidenhead-
based domestic lawnmower manufacturer.

Ransomes is acutely aware of the importance of the European
market to its future and is taking action to be identified as a truly
European company. On its success in exploiting those market opportunities will depend its chances of remaining an independent producer
in the long term. As Sandy Cameron puts it, 'the best chance of
resisting a predator is to maintain our own high performance record'.

At the end of 1987, Ransomes set up its own internal committee to
consider the implications of 1992 for its business. 'The initial task of
finding information was extremely difficult. It was not until I attended
the CBI/*Economist* Conference in 1988 that I had anything other than
the most general ideas of what 1992 was all about.'

The company's 1992 committee has, however, sought to involve all
major parts of the business in planning future developments.
Ransomes is proud of its participative structure and, at regular 'quality
meetings', employees have been involved from the start in discussing
what needs to be done to prepare for the single market. Certain
immediate action points have been identified, such as language
training, which management sees as of key importance.

In the 1980s the market for commercial grass-cutting equipment
has grown rapidly on the continent. Three factors have contributed to
this:

- The increasing number of golf courses

- Greater local authority consciousness of the 'look' of public open space

- The conversion of land from farming to open, recreational purposes

Ransomes is fortunate in being the only European producer of commercial grass-cutting machinery with a complete product range. There are a number of other UK companies, and Dutch and German rivals who all have certain niche strengths particularly in their home markets. Ransomes' main competition comes from US exports by Toro and Jacobsen. These companies dominate the large US market which accounts for over 50 per cent of global demand. In recent years they have, however, come under challenge from the Japanese particularly in the US market, though in the European market the Japanese do not have the full range of products which Ransomes can offer.

Ransomes sees its ability to fight off both US and Japanese competition as dependent on constant improvements and technical innovation, and the pursuit of excellence in the quality of the product it offers. In the commercial market, product reputation is the key – quality, reliability and performance matters more than price. Ransomes has traditionally sold its products through an established dealer network: in France and West Germany, where it was unable to identify a suitable dealer/importer, it set up its own distribution subsidiaries. They have adopted this strategy worldwide, too.

A central strategic question is the company's future relationship with its dealers. Ransomes has traditionally seen itself as a manufacturer, not a distributor – and in the short to medium term it is very dependent on its relationship with its dealers. After 1992 dealers may see opportunities to sell across frontiers: this could cause some awkwardness if price differentials exist between neighbouring countries. Alternatively the dealers may get together, which would increase their market power *vis-à-vis* Ransomes. Or perhaps nothing much will change at all.

The Ransomes franchise, although extremely valuable and much sought after, has never been large enough on its own for dealers to trade comfortably and there is, therefore, the need for complementary products to be sold alongside the Ransomes range. There is the fear that one of Ransomes' existing dealers may be acquired by a competing manufacturer as part of its plans in preparing for 1992. Recognising this danger, Ransomes feels the need to get closer to the 'end-user' in order to keep in touch with changing customer needs and respond faster to them. This may be particularly true when public tendering is eventually liberalised. Local authorities are significant customers of Ransomes, and it is important that they perceive Ransomes as a European company, committed to Europe.

In the domestic lawnmower business, Ransomes' Mountfield subsidiary serves the top end of the consumer market, with no attempt to compete with the 'cheap and cheerful' manufacturers. Ransomes sees particular scope for expansion of Mountfield sales on the continent, particularly in the fast-growing French market where it estimates its existing market share to be no more than 5 per cent. However, in 1988 Ransomes made its first acquisition on the Continent with the purchase of the Italian manufacturer BTS Green in Monza.

The fundamental reason for making this acquisition was that the Mountfield plant at Maidenhead was running close to full capacity. Production was 30 per cent up in the year. Expansion on site was impossible and Ransomes had no desire to start domestic lawnmower production at its main Ipswich factory, which manufactures commercial machinery. So the decision was taken to look for an acquisition in continental Europe. Close links had already been established with Italy because the aluminium castings for the Maidenhead product were manufactured in Italy and in fact were also supplied to the plant which Ransomes decided to purchase.

BTS Green was not the first Italian company Ransomes looked at but it had the advantage of a relatively empty site with plenty of scope for the expansion of local manufacturing. However, the company was family-owned and many cultural differences in attitude and practice emerged in the negotiations.

First, there was some difficulty in interpreting the company's balance sheet. The family's financial affairs were inevitably entwined with the company's, and it was necessary to seek comprehensive warranties before the deal could go ahead. This caused much more of a problem than agreeing the price, which had been arrived at with relative ease, largely because Ransomes already knew the company fairly well.

Second, it was absolutely essential to employ first-class Italian lawyers whom, in Ransomes' case, its own solicitors had recommended. The legal formalities were extremely time-consuming and difficulties occurred in the translation of documents. Detailed handling of local labour contracts was also left to the Italian lawyers.

Third, Ransomes felt it necessary to put in its own Italian manager once the deal went through, though there was no change for change's sake.

Fourth, the deal was a cash one. The vendors were not interested in anything else. Because the amount was small, Ransomes had no problem in funding the deal out of its own resources. However, the

Italian operation is expected to use up quite a bit of capital in the years ahead.

Ransomes, however, was determined to overcome these detailed problems in making an acquisition because it realised its future lies in the European Community. The Italian acquisition was only a first step in the direction of Europeanisation. In November 1988 it acquired Granja, a family company based in Toulouse, which manufactures a range of rotary mowers and other horticultural equipment which can be sold alongside the Mountfield production range. Again the deal was a cash one and the vendor was happy to carry on running the business until a successor could be recruited.

Ransomes used the Paris office of their London solicitors, and Sandy Cameron makes the point, 'These firms are expensive, but the costs are trivial compared to the damage that a badly drawn up deal can do to the profit and loss account. In any future acquisitions we would consider them a key member of our negotiating team.'

III

IMPLEMENTATION

7. Identifying a suitable acquisition target

Making an acquisition on the Continent is one way of expanding across the Channel, and many British companies, both quoted and unquoted, have already chosen this route for expansion. An acquisition may be the best route to achieve the desired ends, particularly if rapid development on the Continent is a high priority. Although each case is different, there are a number of issues which every company seeking to make a Continental acquisition will need to address.

Information sources

Obtaining information about Continental businesses can be extremely difficult. There is no short-cut to industry knowledge, but if the company is not already operating in the target territory, it may have very little useful intelligence.

Some information unreliable

Unfortunately, there is no *Compleat Angler* manual for each member state and business sector. The available information is of inconsistent quality: accounts compiled on unfamiliar bases and sometimes several years out of date; trade and other directories carrying lists which are not exhaustive and often not verified; computer databases which produce figures without giving their source, and which often conflict with each other; national registers detailing property ownership, litigation, filed corporate information, etc., which are often incomplete and poorly maintained; stock exchange filings, but not all stock exchanges are well-regulated; and brokers' research, press and other commentary, much of which will be uneven in its coverage.

All the above sources are, nevertheless, valuable, and often they will be the only practical sources of data. However, the best way for a company to obtain the required information is to retain an expert to find it, particularly as very little of the information obtainable will be in English.

Local knowledge   There is no real substitute for good local intelligence to assist in identifying Continental acquisitions. Some companies appoint local or regional representatives for this purpose. Others adopt a step-by-step approach to identifying acquisition targets, first establishing some form of trading link in the target territory – perhaps selling through an independent distributor or a sales office – before considering any acquisition. Companies like Vickers and Emess have discovered acquisition targets as a result of existing trading links. The companies were known to them. Emess also benefited from on-the-ground knowledge of their local distribution subsidiary. Others took the step of commissioning surveys, having first identified the target market and the kind of business they wanted to acquire. This is how De La Rue, for example, identified the Spanish security printer, Lerchundi.

Agencies   In addition, there are agencies which exist to maintain registers of corporate information. These can, however, be expensive to access and the information they glean is often out of date and frequently unreliable as a true guide to the present situation. Some agencies will undertake specific research projects which can be more useful. This will inevitably be costly, especially where generally available published information is in short supply.

Stockbrokers   The larger UK-based stockbrokers now often research sectors overseas, but their knowlege of smaller businesses will generally be slight – their main concern is to identify and understand the major companies, particularly those which may have a direct impact on the business of UK companies in the relevant sector. Nevertheless, their understanding of what is happening in various business sectors is valuable in helping to point the researcher in the right direction. France, Italy and West Germany are now fairly widely researched, and the resulting reports are in English. A brief telephone conversation is typically free, but more in-depth research will be charged for.

The UK branches of overseas brokers can be useful sources, but their systems and resources will not normally be as extensive as those of their UK counterparts. Accordingly, the amount, reliability and detail available from them may well be inadequate. Moreover, the information they do have will often not be in English.

Both UK and overseas brokers are far more receptive to inquiries from the investing institutions – the key market for their research – so individual companies, especially those wishing to remain anonymous, may have difficulty in gaining more than the most cursory response. Furthermore, it is essential not to alert brokers to the possibility of a company becoming a takeover target.

Equity   As can be seen from Table 7, there is a vast range in the sizes of the equity markets in Europe. The UK has by far the largest, with over 2,500 quoted companies and, of this sample, Belgium is the smallest

Table 7: Size of market and capitalisation: domestic companies								
	Belgium	Denmark	France	Italy	N'lands	Spain	UK	W. Germany
No. of quoted companies (1987)	199	281	383	248	276	328	2542	460
Market capitalisation (£ billion)	26	9	113	97	56	34	370	158

with just under 200. The total value of equities ranges from £9 billion in Denmark to £370 billion in the UK. More surprising, perhaps, are the figures for major economies like France and West Germany, whose markets are valued at just £113 billion and £158 billion respectively, with only around 400 to 500 quoted companies in each market.

One result of the relatively modest size of the Continental equity markets in terms of numbers of companies quoted is that there is a smaller demand for analytical research from brokers than we see in the UK. As there is also a smaller investment community, the investor relations business is not as well developed. Public information on companies is therefore less readily available. There is also more limited information on smaller companies which might be coming to the market than in the UK, as flotations are far less common.

It is possible in most countries to obtain credit agency reports on companies, but these will often be limited. Sales revenues, perhaps several years out of date, numbers of employees, registered addresses, officers and principal locations can commonly be identified once a company is targeted. But, apart from the credit rating itself, these reports will be derived from the public registers.

Financial statements

Upgrading standards

Efforts have been made by the EC authorities to upgrade the filing, accounting and auditing standards throughout the EC. In particular, the Fourth Directive (adopted in 1979) requires annual accounts, including a directors' report and audit opinion, to be published in accordance with the law in each member state; and if the national law does not require publication, the annual report must be available for public inspection free of charge at the company's registered office. Smaller companies are allowed exemptions from some of the requirements, depending on the member state. But some countries (Spain, for example) have yet to comply at all.

In addition, the Seventh Directive (1983) requires the publication of consolidated financial statements. By the end of 1988, many member states had still not even begun to legislate in accordance with this Directive, although a few (including the UK) already comply in practice with its key provisions.

Table 8 shows the current position on the Fourth and Seventh Directives in the six largest (in terms of GDP) member states, in so far as private companies are concerned. There is also a difference in the timing of financial information filing. While the UK is certainly not the fastest in theory, in practice the publicly accessible registers yield far more up-to-date and complete information than in most of the other member states.

Quality of audits

The quality of the information in company accounts depends heavily on the audit procedures. These vary considerably throughout the EC. Prior to the Eighth Directive, auditors only had to be authorised by the applicable national law to carry out their duties. However, the Eighth Directive laid down some major provisions regarding the educational qualifications of those wishing to train as auditors, and the form, length and content of their training. Essentially, auditors may be individuals, partnerships or (in France, West Germany, Italy, Denmark and Portugal) companies. The mini-

Table 8: Filing requirements for private companies			
Member state	Timing of filing after year end	4th Directive enacted	7th Directive enacted
France	7 months	√	×
Italy	5 months	×	×
Netherlands	13 months	√	From 1/1/1990
Spain	No limit	×	×
UK	10 months	√	(Covered by the Companies Bill)
West Germany	9 months	√	From 1/1/1990

mum conditions that auditors must satisfy under the Directive include the following – they must:

- Be of good repute, and not carry out 'incompatible activities'
- Satisfy a test of professional conduct, which should guarantee the 'necessary level' of knowledge
- Possess a general education up to university standard (not necessarily a degree) and have completed at least three years' training

Table 9 shows differing audit practices in the largest EC countries, including whether the Eighth Directive has been enacted. The position varies substantially across the EC. As with most Directives, there are transitional provisions for existing auditors, subject to the discretion

Table 9: Audit requirements			
Country	8th Directive enacted	Independence	Differing audit requirements
France	✗	✓	Small companies need no audit
Italy	✗ (except for listed and some other companies)	Limited	Limited arrangements for private companies
Netherlands	✗	✓	Small companies generally need no audit
Spain	✗	✗	Small companies need no audit
UK	✗ (but covered by the Companies Bill)	✓	None
West Germany	✓	✓	Small companies' auditors need only reduced qualifications

of each member state. Although the Eighth Directive requires some professional integrity, there is as yet no general obligation on auditors to be independent of the companies they are auditing, nor any clear rules as to how audits should be conducted or any specific standards to be applied.

International practice

There are, however, international accounting standards created by the International Accounting Standards Committee. These standards are currently the subject of debate and review and an exposure draft of new proposals is expected early in 1989. If approved, more consistent international rules may come into effect in 1991. The thornier issues include:

- The write-off of goodwill, which the IASC proposes should be written off through the profit and loss account normally over twenty years. This compares with current US practice which allows forty years, whereas in the UK goodwill is typically written off against balance sheet reserves, leaving the profit and loss account unaffected.
- The valuation of inventories where the ISAC advocates FIFO (first in, first out) in line with UK practice whereas, in the USA, LIFO (last in first out) is normally employed.
- Accounting for deferred taxes, where UK companies would have to set aside far larger balance sheet provisions than at present.

The aim of the IASC is to facilitate cross-border comparison of company accounts, but this will clearly take time. Accordingly, great care must be taken in interpreting company accounts. Not only are auditing standards variable, but the accounting standards and practices are themselves highly divergent between even the most sophisticated countries, although steps have already been taken in Brussels to bring in some consistency.

In West Germany, for example, companies cannot revalue their fixed assets – they must always be carried at cost. Similarly, investments are shown at cost. Inventories may either be given at minimum production cost (direct material and labour costs, but excluding overheads or depreciation), or at their maximum value (full production cost, including all overheads and depreciation). Pensions are typically funded through balance sheet provisions allowing only for actuarial assessment of the present value of current pension entitlements. There is no requirement to provide in the accounts for future pension commitments – these could represent considerable off-balance-sheet liabilities. Indeed, pension provisions, being held in the balance sheet, help to fund the working capital of the business.

On the other hand, West German companies have to provide for certain accrued liabilities not necessarily included in UK accounts, such as accruals for repairs and maintenance not carried out in the year under review. Also certain leases are capitalised in the accounts of the lessee in circumstances where this would not be permissible under UK rules.

Because West German accounts can be very difficult to interpret, the Deutsche Vereinigung für Finanzanalyse und Anlageberatung (DVFA) – the West German Association of Financial Analysts – has developed its own yardstick for measuring company profitability on a fully audited accounts basis. The DVFA adjusts the annual net income of AGs (West German public companies) for extraordinary, periodical and special factors, to provide a basis for comparing companies, with a view to giving a clear situation after tax. It is therefore common for major West German companies to file accounts giving one set of information and for informed analysts to work on quite different numbers.

Shareholding details

Degree of disclosure varies

Learning about shareholders is even more problematic. The national filing requirements generally apply only to financial statements. The degree of disclosure of shareholdings required is extremely variable across the EC. Table 10 shows how some countries with extensive financial filing requirements like the Netherlands do not even require publication of major shareholders' details. This is an area where the EC authorities are currently attempting to apply some minimum rules. The first draft of a Directive was provisionally approved by the Council of Ministers in July 1988 and a revised version has been prepared which requires disclosure of holdings over 10 per cent.

Bearer shares

The problem of identifying shareholders is compounded by the prevalent use of bearer, rather than registered, shares on the continent. The use of bearer shares means that, unless the shares are owned by a small group, companies will often not know themselves who their shareholders are, except when the shareholders declare themselves to the company for the purpose of collecting dividends or voting in general meetings.

In the case of publicly quoted companies, information is more readily available than for private companies. This applies just as much elsewhere as in the UK. However, the relative dearth of listed companies on the Continent limits the value of this greater amount of information. Moreover, disclosure by a listed company of share stakes to the authorities will often not be made public (as, for example, in Italy) and the value of such disclosure is therefore limited.

Table 10: Disclosure requirements		
Member state	Quoted companies – public disclosure threshold for shareholdings	All companies – annual publication of shareholdings
France	5%	5%+
Italy	×	10 biggest at AGM only
Netherlands	×	×
Spain	× (with limited exceptions)	× (with limited exceptions)
UK	5%	Full list
West Germany	×	25%

Information on private companies

Even after identifying and approaching the target company, information can be difficult to find. Private, especially family-owned, companies very often have limited understanding of their own relative position in the market. There has been no need for them to review their market's growth potential, nor their competitors' activities except where they affect them directly. It is also common for a family's finances to be entwined with those of the company itself, since there has never been a reason for separation. This is not, of course, peculiar to the Continent. Accordingly, the true profitability and balance sheet position of the company is often unclear to the vendors, let alone to a potential acquirer. Obtaining accurate, reliable and specific information on companies is, therefore, no easy matter. It will often only come to light some time after negotiations have commenced, once the acquiring company's auditors and lawyers have looked very carefully at the real position of the business.

Forms of company ownership

On the Continent, wide ownership of businesses, with people investing for financial returns rather than any particular relationship with the company, is less well established than in the UK. Indeed, institu-

**Investment in
equities**

tional investment in equities is far less developed. For example, in many Continental countries pension funds are managed largely by the banks and are subject only to modest expectations in terms of the returns earned. They concentrate on investment in secure bonds and government stocks. Large equity portfolios are rare, and in the Netherlands, for example, a pension fund with more than about 20 per cent invested in equities is considered very aggressive.

As a consequence, therefore, of the absence of some or all of the UK-style institutional investors, private or controlled public companies are dominant on the Continent.

**Variations in nature
of equity
participation**

Another complicating factor is the wide variety of equity and quasi-equity securities depending on the country. The analysis in Table 11 does not take account of the numerous variants of convertible debt, warrants to subscribe for equity, redeemable securities and other hybrids resulting from financial engineering. Understanding even the basic types of security when undertaking an acquisition can be important in appreciating the real financial position of the target company, and where the true ownership and control of the company lies.

In France, for example, quoted companies tend to issue bearer shares, while unlisted companies are required to have only registered shares. There are also investment certificates representing non-voting ordinary shares, as well as non-voting preference shares.

West German companies generally have bearer shares, though registered shares are permitted. Preferred shares are also not unusual. These are commonly participating, non-voting and cumulative (essentially hybrids of UK-style ordinary and preference shares).

In Italy, ordinary and preferred shares are complemented by non-voting savings shares. All are in registered form, except that fully paid new savings shares may be bearer. Preferred and savings shares may not together account for more than half the total share capital of an Italian company. They can, however, be issued in convertible form. Only listed companies may issue savings shares, which will be in bearer form.

In the Netherlands, public companies (NVs) may have bearer or registered shares, and bearer shares must be fully paid. Private companies (BVs) must have registered shares. In addition to ordinary and preference shares, Dutch '*structuur*' companies (a form of large Dutch company which can leave substantial control in the hands of the management and employees through a supervisory board) can issue priority shares which, *inter alia*, carry the exclusive right to vote on changing the Articles, and tend to be issued in very small numbers. They are normally held by the management or a tightly controlled 'foundation'. *Structuur* companies are therefore essentially bid-proof.

Dutch company shares are typically traded through a system of

Table 11: Types of shares (listed companies)

	Belgium	France	Italy	Netherlands	Spain	UK	West Germany
Regist'd shares	Yes	Yes	Yes	Yes	Yes	Yes	Yes
Bearer shares	Yes*	Yes	Yes*†	Yes*	Yes*	No	Yes
Types of shares	– common – preferred (to dividends and/or liquidation surplus) – beneficiary shares (e.g. to founders for services rendered)	– common – preferred (to dividends and/or liquidation surplus) – shares with double voting rights – non-voting priority (up to 25% of share capital) – investment certificates (up to 25% of share capital)	– common – 'savings shares' (non-voting preferred shares) – shares with limited voting rights (e.g. to vote on resolutions requiring approval at a shareholders' EGM) – (shares with no/limited voting rights restricted to 50% of registered capital) – registered/ bearer bonds	– common – preferred (up to 50% of share capital) – cumulative preferred – priority (exclusive right to vote on appointment/dismissal of directors, amendments to articles of association, etc.) – founders' shares (for services rendered) – non-voting certificates of shares (scrip certificates)	– common – preferred (both with equal voting rights)	– common – preference	– common – preferred (e.g. to dividend) – non-voting (up to 50% of all shares issued) – convertible/ non convertible bonds

* must be fully paid   † only for new non-voting saving shares (Azioni di Risparmio) certificates of deposit of shares. In such cases, the certificates are traded but they carry no votes and may only be convertible into shares in large blocks. These will normally only be exchangeable for ordinary shares at a huge discount to their face value, and the resultant shares may only carry restricted voting rights.

Debt securities

Unusual debt securities flow from different kinds of business practice in the various member states. In West Germany, for example, a widespread form of commercial security is constituted by a transfer of ownership of assets to a creditor (normally a bank), whereby the assets remain in the possession and use of the debtor company. This is called '*Sicherungsübereignung*'. It is also found in the Netherlands as '*fiduciaire eigendomsoverdracht*'. Dutch companies also frequently use debt contracts ('*onderhandse leningen*'), which are not quoted on the stock market, and tend to have a maturity of fifteen to twenty-five years.

French companies have a system of participating loans which are treated as equity by the company. The lenders have last call on the assets of the borrowing company in the event of liquidation or bankruptcy. However, the loan contract may contain a clause entitling the lender to share in the company's profits as well as receiving interest on the loan. In such cases, the lender has priority in distributions of profits. Companies with such loan contracts will often be bound by commitments regarding their commercial and/or industrial activities, reducing the flexibility of the company and its shareholders in the management of the business.

Public ownership

Privatisation

Companies may find acquisition opportunities in the current trend towards privatisations, which are becoming more common on the Continent. Each country has a different approach to this subject. In Italy, for example, state involvement in industry can largely be traced back to the recession in the 1920s and 1930s, when, as in West Germany, the banks found themselves exchanging debt for equity in the hardest-hit businesses. However, in Italy the Legge Bancaria was enacted in 1939 forcing the banks to transfer such equity holdings to IRI, the state holding company and later ENI and EFIM. This law was the original basis for state ownership in Italy, a concept later developed for political reasons. When the state-owned companies required additional financing, the banks began to play an important role again. With the re-emergence of profits in some of the companies, privatisation is now being tentatively pursued.

Much of Italian industry has some degree of public ownership and much of what is wholly private consists of family-owned companies. This leaves a relatively small field of widely owned companies with shareholders separate from the management, where public offers for companies might be practicable.

The problems of buying Italian companies as a result of privatisation are illustrated by the case of SME, the IRI-owned Italian supermarket and foods group, which was put up for auction in 1985. De Benedetti, the Italian industrialist, was successful in the auction. However, IRI then decided not to sell to him after all. Notwithstanding a long court battle which ended only in 1988, SME has been kept in the state sector. It is now seen as a profitable business which can best benefit the state by making acquisitions of its own to build up a powerful force in the industry.

In the UK the Government has already privatised around 40 per cent of the previously state-owned sector. Apart from the pending privatisation of electricity and water, British Coal has been named, and British Rail is being considered. But it is not so much the massive undertakings themselves that are of interest to UK companies, as some of their smaller, ancillary activities. Royal Ordnance, various parts of the Rover Group, and businesses like the Government's Professional Executive Recruitment agency, have all been sold to single corporate purchasers.

Some UK companies have already been active in bidding in other countries, although there is a tendency for such auctions to be relatively private affairs. Certain Spanish building materials interests were, for example, sold to UK companies, while other major UK players only heard of the auction process after the deals had been completed.

Methods of privatisation

Each country adopts its own methods of privatisation. Some prefer auctions, some private deals with one preferred purchaser, and others (less commonly) look to flotation on the stock markets. Very often only minority interests are sold. This can mean a relatively inexpensive entry for the acquiring company, which may hope to buy in the balance at some future date. Selling a minority stake enables the government concerned to raise funds without losing control of the relevant business and also gives the acquiring company or other investors time to assess this new investment.

In the UK, the Government has been careful in many cases of privatisation by flotation to retain rights to itself in order to ensure an orderly transfer of the business into the private sector. Jaguar, Amersham International and others all have golden shares or some other mechanisms to protect against, *inter alia*, single shareholders building up too large a stake for a defined period after privatisation.

Countries with less-developed stock markets are more wary about privatisation by flotation. Indeed, when the Spanish government floated Endesa, the electricity supplier, it was well taken up in London and New York but was poorly received in Spain itself. This caused concern over future attempts to privatise by flotation and the possible effect on the domestic Spanish equity market. For many EC countries, therefore, auctions or single purchaser deals are more likely to be preferred, leading to opportunities for interested corporate buyers.

Foreign ownership   Most governments are extremely sensitive to foreign ownership. 1992 notwithstanding, this is still true of EC countries, and even the British government imposes foreign ownership restrictions when floating previously state-owned assets, although this is now being challenged by the EC authorities in the case of Rolls Royce.

Opportunities for corporate buyers may, therefore, exist in many parts of the Community. In Portugal, for example, constitutional reforms are coming through to allow the full privatisation of state assets. These include a state-owned brewing company and some insurance companies, although the degree of foreign investment which may be allowed has yet to be determined and is likely to be restricted. In Greece, following the elections in 1989, most analysts expect a full-scale privatisation programme, which could include textile and banking interests. In France, on the other hand, the privatisation programme, which saw Société Générale, Matra and others removed from the state sector, has now stalled.

Acquisition criteria

Before undertaking research into possible acquisitions, a company will need to have identified its own acquisition parameters. The more obvious criteria of size, business activity and location may be readily addressed but it is worth taking some time to clarify, in as much detail as may be practicable without creating an impediment to novel ideas, some benchmarks against which to set new acquisition projects. The aim is to save time and wasted effort in the long run, by rapidly filtering out unacceptable proposals for predetermined reasons.

The following checklist sets out the kind of issues which acquiring companies typically look at. Those companies which are frequent acquirers may well use far more sophisticated models.

Proforma acquisition criteria checklist

1. Price range

2. Business activities

3. Location

4. Markets served

5. Performance measures

   - Net sales growth

   - Operating/trading profit growth

   - Operating margins, etc.

   - Interest cover

   - Earnings growth

   - Return on capital

   - Price/earnings historic and forecast (quoted companies)

6. Balance sheet

   - Minorities and non-equity participants

   - Working capital

   - Asset backing

   - Net debt/equity gearing

7. Cash flow

8. Management

   - Continuity post acquisition

   - Linguistic skills

   - Quality, age, etc.

   - Attitude to takeover

   - Need for management strengthening/turnaround

9. Employees

   - Number

   - Unionisation

   - Industrial relations record

10. Market position

    - Leadership, niche, etc.

    - Maturity/growth prospects

    - Marketing/product led

    - Volume/value

    - Competitive pressure

    - Market nature (global, regional, national, etc.)

11. Products

    - Innovative/mature

    - Brands

    - Value added

    - Capital/labour intensive

12. Tax position; availability of tax losses, etc.

Potential acquisitions can be set against these pre-determined requirements. In view of the difficulties outlined above in collating and interpreting information on overseas companies, patently not all the criteria will be capable of full assessment. The checklist, however, essentially acts as a guide for eliminating those which are clearly unsuitable, and no potential acquisition is likely ideally to match the desired parameters in any event. Such a checklist, which should be carefully monitored and modified as both the company and its markets develop, can be a very useful filter and therefore save time.

It is important to emphasise that such criteria are a guide only. An imaginative acquisition idea can release possibilities not previously envisaged, notwithstanding that previously formulated requirements need to be stretched, or perhaps totally rethought, to entertain it.

8. Understanding the regulatory context

A major item in assessing a proposed acquisition is to appreciate the relevant local, regional and supranational regulatory frameworks:

- Competition policy
- Takeover practice
- Exchange controls
- Restrictions on foreign ownership

Competition policy

Competition policy in the EC derives from Articles 85 and 86 of the Treaty of Rome. Article 85 prohibits agreements which affect trade between member states and prevent, restrict or distort competition within the Community. Article 86 prohibits the abuse of a dominant market position in the EC in so far as trade between member states is affected.

Unfair competition   The 1985 White Paper on the single market stressed that it was 'necessary to ensure that anti-competitive practices do not engender new forms of local protectionism which would lead to a repartitioning of the market'. However, it is widely recognised that the intensified competitive environment of the single market will inevitably lead to business combinations and arrangements, and indeed that this may well be desirable to enable EC companies to be internationally competitive against non-EC rivals. There is therefore a need to create a balance between the pragmatic aims underlying the single market and effective measures against anti-competitive agreements.

Commission's powers limited   A key problem is that the Commission's formal powers are essentially limited to intervention *ex-post facto*. There is no established procedure for it to block a bid. It has therefore started to adapt the powers it does have, as for example in the recent bid for Irish Distillers.

In that case, a group of companies (Allied Lyons, Grand Metropolitan and Guinness) combined together to make a consortium bid for Irish Distillers. Their agreement provided that they should not compete with each other in bidding for the target, and that they would divide up the acquired business between them. The Commission had no power to block the bid, but intervened with interim measures suspending the bid on the grounds that the agreement between the purchasers was anti-competitive. Further progress by the bidders was thereby inhibited and the consortium bid was withdrawn.

Powers of investigation

The Commission has fairly wide powers of investigation, although it has no power to issue a search warrant as such. Nevertheless, the Commission's officers can call at premises without notice and demand records. In general, however, it relies heavily on being consulted, and is ready to give comfort letters in specific cases which are not already covered by block exemptions previously established.

The main sea change in the Commission's attitude is seen in its aim to bring mergers and acquisitions squarely within the scope of EC competition policy. Until recently, its interpretation of Article 85 was that it did not apply to agreements to buy all or part of the ownership of a company or its underlying assets. Article 86 was considered only relevant to mergers and acquisitions if they increased market dominance which was abused. In 1987, however, the European Court ruled that Article 85 does include agreements to buy shares in a competitor, in that this could result in a change in the competitive behaviour of the companies concerned. It is, however, still unclear how far this goes and, although the Commission takes the view that the purchase of a controlling interest in a competitor is now covered under Article 85, this has yet to be tested.

De minimis rules

In any event, many acquisitions will come below the *de minimis* rules laid down by the Commission. These apply if the goods and services covered, or apparently covered, by the agreement (i.e. for one company to acquire the other) comprise no more than 5 per cent of the relevant part of the EC market for those goods and services and the combined turnover of the companies does not exceed 200 million ecus (about £130 million). However, as the definition of the appropriate market is often a matter for debate, companies cannot always be confident of being exempt.

Proposed merger control regulation

At the time of writing, EC competition procedures are in a state of flux. Attempts are being made to obtain approval from the Council of Ministers to a regulation on merger control. (Regulations are a direct form of legislation from Brussels, not requiring enabling legislation by the member states.) If adopted as presently drafted, it will represent a major development in competition rules in that large EC mergers and acquisitions will in some respects be exclusively reviewed by the Commission, not national bodies or governments.

The present proposal would give the Commission exclusive rights to block or clear mergers and acquisitions where EC competition is affected and where the combined annual turnover of the companies involved exceeds 1 billion ecus (about £650 million) worldwide. A suggestion was made by the Commission to increase this limit to 2 billion ecus, but as yet the 1 billion ecu threshold is still part of the formal proposal. The Commission would also only be concerned with cases where the aggregate Community turnover of at least two of the relevant companies is more than 100 million ecus. However, where each of the companies achieves at least three quarters of their aggregate Community turnover in one member state, the transaction would be left to the national authorities.

It is interesting to note that, as proposed at present, clearance by the Commission would be conclusive: national governments would not then be able to intervene on competition grounds. They may, however, retain the right to intervene for reasons of national interest, such as defence, control of media, and entry into certain supervised businesss like banking and insurance.

The threshold for this proposed regulation as drafted at the time of writing is high enough not to affect most acquisitions. There is also continuing debate on the criteria which the Commission should apply under the Regulation. However, the Commission will retain powers under Articles 85 and 86 and these powers could affect a company when buying, or entering into any significant arrangement with, a business in another member state, or even within the same country if the deal could affect trade between member states. If there is any doubt about the position, the Commission should be approached before the transaction is completed.

Importance of domestic competition rules

Until the EC-wide position is finally clarified, and even afterwards for deals outside the proposed regulation's scope, national competition rules are still an important factor, particularly in the UK, West Germany, France and the Republic of Ireland where effective controls already exist. Other member states are developing national controls of their own. Table 12 gives an overview of national competition rules in the six largest member states. The following examples illustrate the diversity of national competition rules in the Community.

In West Germany, the anti-trust laws provide for advance notification of a proposed merger to the Cartel Office, which has one month to advise that it has started inquiries and four months to decide on the merger. Advance notice is mandatory when each of the companies has an annual turnover of over DM 1 billion (approximately £320 million), or if either has an annual turnover of over DM 2 billion (approximately £640 million). The Cartel Office generally blocks the merger if it creates a dominant position in the market. In 1985 some

Table 12: National competition rules			
Country	National rules	Criteria warranting investigation	Pre-notification required
France	✓	Market share (25%) and turnover thresholds	✗
Italy	✗	✗	✗
Netherlands	✓	Public interest	✗
Spain	✗	✗	✗
UK	✓	Market share (25%) and gross assets thresholds	✗
West Germany	✓	Market share (20%) and turnover thresholds	✓

700 mergers and acquisitions were referred, of which 16 per cent involved a proposed acquisition of a West German company by a foreign company. Only seven cases were refused, one involving a foreign company. In 1986, there were 800 referrals, 16 per cent again regarding proposed acquisitions by foreign companies, but only two refusals (neither by foreign companies). In certain sectors, such as media, the level of turnover at which reference to the Cartel Office is mandatory is significantly lower.

In France, the Conseil de la Concurrence (Competition Council) may examine bids which result in the creation of market shares in excess of 25 per cent or sales in excess of 7 billion francs (approximately £640 million).

In the Netherlands, domestic competition rules are laid down in the Economic Competition Act 1958 (*Wet Economische Mededinging*) or WEM). The WEM does not require the parties to a takeover to seek advance clearance. However, if a dominant market position is created which is found by the government to conflict with the general public interest, obligations can be imposed such as a requirement to sell goods or services at prices determined by the relevant minister. In addition, agreements between companies to restrict competition are also subject to government regulation.

In the Republic of Ireland, notification to the Examiner of Restrictive Trade Practices is required of any proposed merger or takeover. As a result of the report and a possible inquiry which may follow, the Irish government may prohibit the takeover, or impose conditions.

It is clear, therefore, that competition policy can be an important factor throughout the EC, both at national and Community level. For the most part acquisitions will be below the relevant thresholds, although notification procedures may apply nevertheless. It is, however, important to assess at an early stage the competition implications of a proposed acquisition, to enable the deal to be so arranged as to avoid difficulties, and ensure that any necessary submissions are made to the relevant authorities. Where optional pre-notification is possible, as for example in the UK, it is normally prudent to take advantage of this, even if formal clearance is not given as a result.

Takeover practice

No uniform set of procedures

There are wide differences in takeover practice throughout the EC. These reflect in part the pattern of company ownership and regulatory controls. But there are also cultural variations which have to be understood for an acquisition to succeed: attitudes to hostile takeovers (or selling out at all); attitudes to foreign investment and management; attitudes to trades unions; and the readiness of different governments to intervene. For example, disclosure of substantial equity stakes in quoted companies varies between the member states (see Table 10). In addition, the first version of a Directive which has been provisionally approved by the Council of Ministers proposes disclosure at levels of either 10 per cent, 20 per cent, 33.3 per cent, 50 per cent and 66.67 per cent or 10 per cent, 25 per cent, 50 per cent and 75 per cent at the member state's discretion.

It should also be noted that, at the time of writing, the UK government has recently announced changes to the disclosure requirements for UK public companies, reducing the threshold for disclosure to 3 per cent and the deadline for disclosing to two days.

In France, tender and exchange offers are governed by the rules of the Stockbrokers Association and the Commission des Opérations de Bourse (COB). Both offeror and offeree have to make filings with the authorities, who may attach conditions to the proposed takeover. There are rules regarding increasing bid values and standards of basic fairness.

In the Netherlands, there is a merger code without legal force. If the code is breached, details are published and reprimands given. The Amsterdam Stock Exchange can also apply sanctions such as suspending quotations and prohibiting members of the Exchange from participating in a prohibited public offer.

Belgium requires notification of mergers and acquisitions and the Minister of Finance must give prior authorisation to public offers for the purchase or exchange of Belgian securities made by or on behalf of Belgian individuals or private companies based abroad or controlled from abroad. If the authorisation is refused, participation in the offer is prohibited.

Impact of different practices

A good example of the impact of differences in takeover practice are the contrasting experiences of Emess and Pernod Ricard. When Emess (the UK lighting company) topped a bid by Thorn–EMI for Holophane (its French counterpart), with the backing of Holophane's board, it had not counted on two peculiarities of French regulatory procedure. First, the French authorities ruled that irrevocable acceptances to the offer (Emess had over 50 per cent) during a bid period were unacceptable, as they prevented shareholders from accepting a possible higher offer. This rule does not apply in the UK. Second, the French stock exchange authority, the COB, refused to register the Emess offer as it was conditional on approval of the associated rights issue at an EGM a few weeks later, even though Emess had irrevocable undertakings from a majority of its shareholders to vote in favour.

These problems allowed Thorn–EMI to come in with a higher bid, which was registered by the COB before the Emess bid. The rules then required Emess to offer a price which exceeded Thorn's bid by 5 per cent, even though Emess still had the recommendation of the Holophane board for its original bid. In the event, Emess withdrew.

In contrast, the French drinks company Pernod Ricard succeeded in its bid for Irish Distillers following rulings that irrevocable acceptances were permissible, despite the fact that a higher rival bid had already been made by Grand Metropolitan.

Public takeover activity

The volume of merger and acquisition activity varies considerably between markets. In the UK, company takeovers, both public and private, are a regular and active feature, much more so than elsewhere in the EC. This is perhaps the biggest contrast between the cultural attitudes of the UK and Continental countries, especially in respect of hostile takeover bids. These are extremely rare on the Continent. And in view of the relatively small number of quoted companies there, even agreed public offers for shares are unlikely to become as common as they are in the UK.

In any event, many quoted Continental companies can take effective action to frustrate unwelcome approaches by would-be bidders. In West Germany, for example, the only successful hostile acquisition to date was by the Swiss Inspectorate Group of the Dortmund-based Harpener in 1987. In fact, no public offer was made. A quarter of the equity was first acquired from a single purchaser, and further purchases were made through the market. But this was not a hostile bid in the same way as those seen in the UK.

In the Netherlands, there have been only three hostile takeover bids attempted, all of which failed. Every listed Dutch company has some constitutional mechanism for protecting its management against predators. The Amsterdam Stock Exchange has recently failed in its attempt to make significant changes to this, and major progress is now unlikely, at least in the short term. One mechanism is the use of certificates of deposit. These certificates alone are traded, carry no voting rights and, although convertible into voting shares, the resultant voting rights will still typically be very limited. Another form of protection is the right in certain cases for the supervisory board to issue new shares freely into friendly hands when threatened by a predator. In the face of such impenetrable fortifications, hostile bids are, to all intents and purposes, ruled out at present.

In Italy the first hostile bid was made in 1971. Although unsuccessful, it established some broad rules of conduct regarding public offers in Italy. These have never been formulated into hard and fast practices. In any event, the fact that Italian equity markets are relatively small and illiquid presents a formidable obstacle to hostile bidders. The first successful public offer was in the early 1980s when Quaker Oats of the USA made an agreed bid for the Italian food company, Chiari e Forte.

The Takeover Directive

In view of the substantial differences in takeover practice, the EC authorities are currently drafting a Directive to cover public takeover procedures throughout the EC. Its effect, regardless of its content, is unlikely to be widely felt in that so few public offers take place on the Continent for reasons quite unconnected with the national rules, or absence of rules, on conducting takeover bids. The Directive, at the time of writing, is being drafted by the Commission. Its object is to try to bring some sort of unity to the way in which takeovers are conducted throughout the EC. The Commission is seeking to establish a co-ordinated legislative framework to create a compatible set of procedures, particularly where a company in one member state or from outside the EC is offering for a company in another.

Each member state will take the legislative framework of the Directive and adapt it to its own circumstances. It is therefore likely that each EC country will still have its own individual system based on the structure and rules required by the Directive. The nature of these will reflect both the varying corporate and market structures and the level of takeover activity experienced. For example, where bearer shares are common, an offer is likely to be notified to shareholders primarily by public advertisement; whereas in the UK, where shares are normally registered, direct mailing is more appropriate as the principal medium of communication. The effect of such differences is already being addressed by the Commission in its proposals, but the differences themselves are more fundamental and less susceptible to harmonisation.

Perhaps the most important aspect of the current proposals is that each country is likely to be required to implement the provisions of the Directive through legally binding rules.

The City Code

In the UK, the long-standing City Code on Takeovers and Mergers is non-statutory. Self-regulation, however, is a concept somewhat alien to many of the other EC member states. One possible outcome is that the Directive could set down some minimum rules, and allow a member state to create whatever system beyond those minimum obligations it chooses.

The Draft Directive deals with the timetable of a bid, supervisory bodies and location of the bidder, the accuracy of statements made, rival offers, publication of the details of the offer and defence arguments, the treatment of acceptances, what happens when the offer is increased and the procedure for dealing with minorities once the bidder gains control. It remains to be seen whether it will in its final form include matters such as bid-triggering stakes requiring a share buyer to make a full offer for all the company's shares; and rules which govern profit and other forecasts, concert parties and loosely connected shareholder groups and certain kinds of frustrating action by the target company's board.

The Commission aims for a final form of the Directive to be adopted by the Council of Ministers by late 1989 or early 1990, with a view to its implementation in most member states by 1992. Its requirements may be different in some respects from those already applied in the UK, but it is unlikely to be onerous for UK takeover practitioners who already have to deal with similar detailed rules, provided that the current flexibility of the UK self-regulatory system is not excessively restricted.

Exchange controls

Existing exchange controls to be dismantled

Exchange controls are still a factor in some parts of the Community. At present France, Italy, Portugal, Spain, the Republic of Ireland and Greece all have some controls in place. But the Council of Ministers has agreed that such controls will be dismantled by 1992, although Portugal, Spain and Greece do have the right to defer compliance.

West Germany has no exchange controls. However, there are reporting requirements on a no-name basis to itemise income received from, and expenditure paid, outside West Germany. In particular, if a foreign investor acquires more than 25 per cent of a West German company's equity, this has to be notified to the company and to the Cartel Office. No attempt is made to control flows of funds.

In Italy, major changes were made on 1 October 1988, as a first step towards complete de-regulation of banking and investment, to comply with EC rules by 1992. These developments show the influence of the single market programme on previously highly controlled areas.

Article 67

The removal of exchange controls within the Community dates back to Article 67 of the Treaty of Rome, which requires progressive abolition of restrictions on the movement of capital by residents of the member states. It has been further extended by the Directive on liberalisation of capital movements in June 1988 which widened the scope of the existing freedom of movement of capital to investments in short-term securities, current and deposit account banking operations and financial loans and credits.

Restrictions on foreign ownership

Withholding tax

Various forms of restriction still exist in the Community. Dividends and interest receivable from overseas companies are, for example, generally subject to withholding tax. As can be seen from Table 13,

Table 13: Withholding tax

	France	Italy	Netherlands	Spain	UK	West Germany
Dividends – rate of withholding tax for non-residents	25% except for foreign recipients who may receive relief from tax treaties (UK 15%)	32.4% on ordinary + 15% on savings shares – rates may be reduced with double taxation agreements (UK 5% to 15% depending on level of ownership)	25% paid by resident and non-resident, except foreign recipients may receive further relief under tax treaty (UK 15%, or 5% if more than 25% of shares owned)	20% unless reduced by tax treaty (UK 10% if more than 10% of shares owned)	15% or 5% where dividends paid with tax credit or half tax credit respectively	25% except if reduced by double taxation already (UK 15%, or 20% if controlling shareholding)

115

standard withholding taxes range from 15 per cent in the UK (although this is not a withholding tax as such) to 32.4 per cent in Italy, and are governed by double taxation treaties between the countries.

There are no other specific restrictions on foreign ownership in West Germany. In France, the position is similar for EC investors, with the exception of the defence industry. In Italy, foreign investment is controlled in a few sectors, such as banking, insurance, air transport and shipping. The Netherlands has restrictions for certain defence related industries, banks and insurance companies, where consent is required from the authorities.

Spain has restrictions on foreign ownership in several industrial sectors, including gambling, defence, broadcasting and airlines. In these cases, specific approval is required. Moreover, the Department of Economy and Taxation has to be informed in advance of any proposed investment from abroad, but approval is automatically given if not informed to the contrary within 30 days. Foreign investment in banks needs prior authorisation from the Spanish Central Bank, except for investments up to 15 per cent in newly established banks. All foreign investments have to be registered with the Spanish authorities to enable funds to be repatriated subsequently.

In the UK, no general restrictions apply. In practice defence and other strategic industries can be protected from foreign investment on national interest grounds. There are additionally rules covering areas such as banking and media. The Bank of England, for example, would withdraw the necessary licences for carrying on banking activities if it did not approve of a bank's owners, domestic or foreign. Privatised companies are also normally protected through golden shares or other restrictions in their Articles.

The single market programme is plainly having a significant impact on the regulatory context for acquisitions in the Community:

- Competition policy is undergoing a major review, and the direct involvement of the European Commission in merger control is already becoming a fact

- There are wide variations in takeover practice in the Community, but proposals to introduce some common rules are well advanced

- Exchange controls are generally due to be removed within the Community by 1992

- Restrictions on foreign ownership will continue in sensitive sectors, but have already been removed in most other areas

9. Doing the deal

Having identified a target company and established as much about it as possible from published and other third party sources, the next stage is to do the deal. In Continental markets, hostile acquisitions of quoted companies are a rarity and this chapter therefore concentrates on the key issues for an agreed acquisition of a controlled company. These are:

- Organising for acquisition

- Making the approach

- Handling negotiations

- Valuation

- Form of consideration

- Managing currency risk

- Management issues

- Handling industrial relations

- Necessary commitment

Organising for acquisition

Making an acquisition is normally very time-consuming for management and advisers alike. Some larger companies have commercial directors, part of whose function is to handle such acquisitions, together with their specialist in-house teams of analysts, auditors, lawyers, and the like. For most acquiring companies this is a luxury, especially where acquisitions are not a constant feature of their corporate development. For these companies senior management resources can be significantly deflected from their other responsibilities when considering possible acquisitions. Certainly, much time-consuming work is often handled by the company's financial adviser, but this does not release the company's own executives from the task of assessing all the implications, preferences and possibilities.

Two particular points are relevant in the case of overseas acquisitions.

- Language difficulties
- The need for good locally based advice

The most obvious difficulty is communication with the vendors and others. Speaking the vendors' language is a social courtesy which can be very helpful in establishing confidence and good relations. But there is an important caveat. Those negotiating complex or particularly critical issues should keep to their native language, unless they are fluent linguists. In these circumstances, local representatives and trusted advisers come into their own simply as channels of communication.

Good local professional advice (regardless of the linguistic aspect) is essential. It is self-evident that lawyers have to understand the local legal system: agreements will almost invariably be covered by the laws of the target company's territory.

Particular care needs to be taken not to enter unintentionally into legally binding arrangements. It does not take much to create a contract and, short of that, written or even oral representations made early on can often result in a contractual obligation.

Moreover, as accounting and audit practices vary widely throughout the Community, while the multinational accountancy firms will be able to cope, other accountants who normally advise the UK company may not. The services of large firms of solicitors and accountants can be expensive: but nothing like as expensive as a bad acquisition.

Not all merchant banks are geared up to advise on Continental acquisitions, so it is important to choose one that is active in this area, preferably with local representatives around Europe. As financial advisers, they play a leading role, not just in identifying the target company, but also in the valuation, negotiation and (where appropriate) coordination and handling of UK and other Stock Exchange requirements, monopolies and mergers representations, funding arrangements and general strategic advice.

Management issues   A fundamental issue the company must address at an early stage is the management resources it can itself bring to bear to manage the acquisition after the deal has been completed. Clearly, different levels of resource are required for small and large acquisitions, and for companies in existing or new areas. Even large companies refuse to enter into negotiations unless they feel confident of being able to manage the company effectively.

The question of post-acquisition management is also important in terms of setting the acquisition criteria. It may well be that the aim is to create a bridgehead in the new territory on which to build further acquisitions. The availability of strategically thinking senior managers with a local appreciation of the whole group's ambitions can be a key consideration.

Making the approach

In making an approach, there are some general principles to follow regardless of the nationality of the target company, and these gain greater significance in a foreign acquisition.

- Gain trust

- Be open

- Ensure confidentiality

The most important of these is to gain the confidence both of the owners and, perhaps later, the management and employees of the business. This can be absolutely fundamental to whether any potential vendor is prepared to enter into negotiations at all and is emphasised time and again in the case studies. A good local representative can be extremely useful in winning the confidence of potential vendors and their management colleagues. De La Rue, for example, attributes the achievement of its Lerchundi acquisition in Spain to the active presence of its own regional director.

The key to winning trust is to be open about intentions. A tentative and mysterious buyer takes away a key ingredient in building up confidence – mutual trust. Vendors can hardly be expected to open up to people who are not prepared to be clear about their intentions and the nature and ambitions of their own business. Shrouded inquiries can be mistaken for undercover investigations by the taxation authorities and this could easily create an unfriendly response to any approach.

However, casual and unguarded approaches to quoted companies are to be avoided, even if the approach is intended to be friendly. The result could well be premature market interest, either as a result of official statements by the target, or following leaks. This creates tension, expectations, a probable increase in the value of the target's shares and a possible reduction in those of the intended buyer. This may force a formalisation of matters much earlier than intended and perhaps sooner than is possible in the circumstances, and may result in abandonment of the proposed transaction.

Buyer's intentions for business

Being open extends not only to the nature of the approach, but also to the buyer's intentions regarding the business, its management and employees, and how it proposes to deal with the business after the acquisition. A well-established family company, for example, may certainly be pleased to learn that the family name of the business is to be retained. If this is not to be the case, and the fact is likely to come out at some point before the acquisition is completed, then it is as well to be frank about it and explain why. Often it is necessary to sell the whole concept of why the acquisition makes sense, and why changing the name is part of the strategy. Castrol, on the other hand, finds that one of its attractions to vendors is the idea of adding the Castrol name to their acquired brand. This concept is sold as the best way to develop wider markets for what were hitherto local products and consequently to build up the vendors' business far beyond what could otherwise be achieved.

Future of existing management and employees

Being open about intentions for management and employees can be more problematic. Owner-managers may be prepared to be reasonably phlegmatic about losing their jobs, as their motivation for selling may be that they want to leave the business in any event. Indeed, some companies make it a rule that managers who suddenly find themselves without a major financial interest in the commercial success of the business and with a sizeable sum in their bank account, should not be retained except, perhaps, on a non-executive basis.

A useful technique is to retain the senior vendor-manager as a non-executive consultant. This helps to preserve continuity in the business, enhances the morale of other continuing managers and maintains customer confidence at a critical time. It also gives the acquiring company the opportunity to pick the brains of someone who may have built up the business in the first place. Both Vickers and Emess have found it useful to retain vendor-managers in a consultative, non-executive role. The relief from having to cope with the day-to-day headache of managing the business can, as in the Emess case study, leave the vendors free to concentrate on their real skills.

But, if the incumbent management is, in whole or in part, unsatisfactory to the buyer, then a judgement has to be made at an early stage as to how ruthless the incoming owner should appear. If the vendors are distinct from the managers, then they may prefer to leave such issues to be dealt with after the acquisition. It may, however, be easier to broach the subject with such vendors as it will not affect them directly. They may welcome the opportunity to forewarn the relevant managers and could be very helpful in saving upset later on.

The gradualist approach

While it may be possible to seize the right moment with an early offer to buy the target company, it is far more likely that the confidence of the vendors will be won by a gradualist approach. Just how this is achieved depends on the circumstances. It may be feasible, for example, to start with a trading relationship as discussed earlier. Or, if the idea of selling out altogether is not attractive to the vendors (or if it is judged that this is likely to be the case), a more acceptable, though more complicated, approach could be to take a minority interest initially, with a view eventually to buying in the balance at a later date.

Inviting the vendors to view the UK company's existing operations and meet the UK management patently displays openness and friendliness. It may be possible to raise the possibility of technology or personnel transfer, demonstrating at the start that value can be added by the combination of the businesses. In any event, taking advantage of opportunities to build up contact with the target company is a clear way of winning confidence and trust.

Confidentiality

A key ingredient for successful negotiations is to assure confidentiality on both sides. Before information is handed over by a company, it has to be confident that the recipient will deal with it responsibly. Normally vendors will require all the relevant principals and advisers to sign confidentiality undertakings, which will include obligations not to copy the information, and not to distribute it beyond a defined group of people without consent. They will also contain restrictions against competing and, in the case of quoted companies, making a hostile offer for a prescribed period. While negotiating these preliminary agreements can be tiresome, they can assume unexpected importance if negotiations break down.

Moreover, it can be desirable from the vendors' point of view to feel free to disclose as much information as possible. The more confident they can make the purchaser regarding their business and its future, the higher the price that can be safely offered: or, at least, retentions against possible warranty claims in the future may be reduced. This is, therefore, a strong reason for vendors to want to be able to trust a purchaser.

Handling negotiations

Issues involved in making the approach naturally overlap with those relating to negotiations. The relationship of trust and openness needs to be sustained throughout the negotiations. However, it is important to appreciate that companies on the Continent are, generally speaking, less familiar with the concept of company takeovers than UK companies. They and their advisers are likely to be uncertain about some aspects of conducting negotiations. In De La Rue's acquisition of Lerchundi, for example, the company's owners had to be guided through the principles of valuation, so that they could be confident that they were being offered a fair deal. Whereas, in Ransomes' acquisition of BTS Green, the negotiation of comprehensive warranties was much more of a problem than agreeing the price.

Where the acquiring company is quoted, there may well be a need under Stock Exchange rules publicly to disclose information about the acquired company which its former owners have always considered completely private: not just audited financial records, but also, for example, details of commercial contacts which directors may have with the company. Moreover, where the acquisition is large relative to a quoted UK company, it may well require prior approval by the UK shareholders and this would mean public disclosure of such matters before the acquisition is even approved.

Differences in funding techniques

UK companies, especially if quoted, tend to use more sophisticated techniques than their Continental counterparts, which may therefore have to be explained. In West Germany, for example, commercial loans from banks up to extremely high gearing levels are commonly the only real source of funding, whereas UK-quoted companies will often look for ways of using equity and various forms of debt securities, as well as hybrids of the two, to fund acquisitions.

While this may not impact directly on the continental vendors, there will be occasions when they have to be party to arrangements which they will never have seen before. It may perhaps be desirable for the UK company to issue shares as consideration for the acquisition which, for accounting reasons, have to be issued directly to the vendors. Assuming (as will probably be the case) that the vendors want their consideration in cash, it is normal to arrange a vendor placing, so that the shares issued to them are immediately placed with willing holders of the UK company's equity. This procedure can seem very complex and worrying for vendors and needs to be carefully explained to allay their concerns.

Valuation

The central element in any negotiation is the determination of a price for the business. Valuing a company is, to say the least, an imprecise art.

Price variables

This is even more so when crossing national boundaries. Moreover, the same business will be worth different amounts to different purchasers. For example, a company with unutilised tax losses in a particular country which it cannot offset may place a higher value on a company with taxable profits in that country than can a rival purchaser not in that position. A company wishing to enter a market with high entry costs may well be prepared to pay a higher premium than a company already operating in that market.

Furthermore, values of otherwise similar businesses vary between countries for a variety of reasons, including potential for market growth, land and other values, and regulatory differences. A standard means for valuing companies, by comparing them to other similar companies, may not be available, either because of the absence of suitable comparisons, or the absence of the valuation benchmarks themselves – relevant price earnings and/or cash-flow ratios, prices achieved in similar previous acquisitions, etc.

In the UK, one can fairly readily and reliably derive the net worth of a company from its balance sheet, the cash flow from the source and application of funds statement, the margins from the profit and loss account, and there are many other audited and easily interpreted figures of value to an acquirer. On the Continent, however, in view of the problems described earlier in interpreting financial accounts, the relevant figures may not be available until detailed investigations have been carried out.

Valuations have to be made, notwithstanding the difficulties, although usually these are conditional on a full audit of the business. Accordingly, it is far from uncommon for the price paid for an acquisition to be based on a balance sheet formula, depending on stock counts and valuations, independent assessment of property and other asset values, tax assessments, order book verification, and so on. Alternatively, a firm price can be set for an agreed minimum value and a deferred element of the consideration can be made dependent on audit, warranty claims, or even future profits over a defined period (earn-outs). Earn-outs are quite common on the Continent as they provide an incentive to vendors who remain managing the business and reduce the initial payment.

Added importance of warranties and indemnities

Warranties and indemnities are common features of all equity sale and purchase agreements, and they acquire even more importance where the valuation of the business is based on sources not independently audited, as will not infrequently be the case with Continental acquisitions. Dealing with this is often the hardest aspect of an acquisition, and the store of mutual trust can be all-important. The vendors may take the view that asking for warranties of the information provided, and indemnities if it turns out to be wrong, is tantamount to a lack of trust in them, or even to accusing them of bad faith.

A purchaser needs to explain that this is normal business practice, and is really a means of identifying what the purchaser has already seen for itself, and what it has not, perhaps revealing areas where the vendors could usefully supply further information. The details of warranties and indemnities are generally best left for the advisers to hammer out but, as an issue, they cannot be avoided. One of our case study interviewees told us that, where the scale of requested warranties and indemnities is challenged, they show the vendors what a US company once required of them, and that normally solves the problem.

Form of consideration

Broadly speaking, there are three ways to pay: in kind, in shares or in cash.

Payment in kind is the most unusual. This would normally involve an asset swap. An example of this occurred in 1987 with Thomson of France and General Electric of the USA. Thomson took over GE's RCA Consumer Electronics business in exchange for Thomson's CGE medical equipment subsidiary. Also, in the UK in 1988, Burnett & Hallamshire bought Anglo United's UK coal business and took on £20 million of debt, in exchange for two Burnett & Hallamshire subsidiaries. Transactions of this kind are very much *sui generis*. They will involve particular difficulties and solutions which defy general rules, and require specific advice in each case.

Cash is the normal consideration for Continental acquisitions. But this does not mean that a quoted company cannot use its own quoted equity, either to raise funds or as direct consideration, although it will then meet problems not encountered in domestic deals. Apart from the technical problems accompanying any issue of shares by a listed UK company, other key factors include:

- Local national regulations restricting the issue of UK shares to non-UK vendors

- The level of understanding of UK fund-raising practices mentioned earlier

The use of the acquirer's shares as consideration may present difficulties for the vendors. Generally, there will be some resistance to holding a foreign company's shares. This will be aggravated by the holding of a sterling asset (i.e. UK shares) creating an exchange risk for the vendors. Moreover, as non-resident UK shareholders, there may be additional taxation complications, depending on the particular taxation agreements between the UK and the jurisdiction of their residence.

Share structures

In addition, the complicated nature of Continental companies' share structures may make a share exchange impractical. The widespread use of bearer shares elsewhere in the EC suggests that exchanging these for UK-registered shares may not appeal to such shareholders unless converted into bearer form. Nevertheless, share exchanges have formed the basis of certain transactions, such as the purchase by the UK property company, Mountleigh, of Galerias Preccados in Spain.

Personal tax considerations can, however, make a share exchange worth considering. The most usual manifestation of this in the UK is that vendors who accept a consideration comprising shares in the purchasing company are normally able to roll over any liability to tax on the capital gain achieved into the new equity or other securities issued. The tax bill is still there to be paid, but it falls due only when the new shares are sold. This ability to defer a tax payment is valuable to the vendors, who may be prepared to take this into account in agreeing the sale price.

Tax rates vary

There is a wide variation between tax rates in the EC, as can be seen from Table 14 which shows the current corporation and capital gains tax rates applicable in selected member states. Taxation differences therefore clearly affect the appropriate value to be placed on a business in different parts of the EC, as well as the value to vendors of the consideration received.

The position of overseas vendors will naturally depend on their own country's taxation rules and whether they are permitted to accept foreign shares and obtain roll-over relief. This form of consideration was used by De La Rue in a recent Dutch acquisition, but for the most part Continental vendors are unlikely to want to be paid in unfamiliar shares quoted and traded only in London.

Managing currency risks

As cash is by far the most common and acceptable form of consideration on the Continent, this raises currency issues when overseas assets are being acquired. Delays are a problem because of the inherent difficulties of cross-border negotiations, especially in view of the potential foreign exchange movements. Taking account of changes in the value of the target business from initial agreement to completion is often a reason for using a balance sheet formula based on an audit

Table 14: Tax rates						
	France	Italy	Netherlands	Spain	UK	W. Germany
Corporation tax	42% on French sourced profits	36%	35%	35%	35% (25% in certain circumstances where income is below £150,000)	56% on resident corporations on retained earnings; 36% on distributed earnings; flat rate of 50% on non-resident corporation
Corporate tax on capital gains	42% on short-term gains (less than 2 years) otherwise 15%	36%	35%	35%	35%	56%
Individual tax on capital gains	Varied rules and rates depending on type of asset	Not taxable unless a business disposal – then taxed at marginal rate (highest 62%)	Not taxable unless a business disposal – then taxed at marginal rate (highest 72%)	Taxable at marginal rate (highest 56%)	Taxable at marginal rate (highest 40%)	Long term not taxable – short term at marginal rate (highest 56%). Individuals have 50% tax relief on the sale of substantial shareholdings; this relief will be abolished from 1/1/90

carried out subsequently – checking stock movements, changes in debtors, creditors, cash, etc. This is just as much an issue within the UK as for an overseas acquisition. But, with foreign acquisitions, once a price has been agreed, the acquiring company should seek to protect itself against relative currency movements. This is all the more important since the UK is not currently part of the exchange-rate mechanism of the European Monetary System.

If there is a one-off cash payment – to take the simplest case – which currency applies? If it is the vendors' currency, then the fact that a UK purchasing company is accounting for this in sterling leaves it open to a clear exchange risk. If the consideration is to be paid in sterling, the vendors are at risk. Either way, the purchaser or the vendors should consider hedging against adverse exchange-rate movements. This need present little problem, and can be made as flexible as required. In broad terms, the aim is to finance the deal at minimum cost and at the same time limit the exposure to foreign currency and the risk of adverse exchange-rate movements.

Hedging

As regards raising finance in the local currency the acquiring company may have no real or immediate need for additional borrowings. It may well have perfectly adequate funds at home to cover the cost of the acquisition. Under these circumstances, it may be as well to consider some re-financing into the local currency.

Local funding

The alternative to local funding is to undertake a money market transaction to create an effective, if not natural, hedge. The key mechanisms are currency swaps off-balance-sheet, parallel loans, or long-dated forward contracts. Each of these can achieve the desired effect and each has merits and disadvantages depending on the precise circumstances.

Currency swaps essentially match, through the market, borrowers with different and complementary problems. The acquiring company takes out a loan in sterling, but through the market it will behave as though the loan were taken out in the desired foreign currency. Virtually any major currency can now be swapped with ease.

Currency swaps

Parallel loans are similar operations, except that the obligations and defaults on one side are not necessarily off-settable against the other side. Typically, the UK company will deposit the borrowed sterling with a bank, which will then lend the company the required local currency, the bank having taken out a parallel loan in the foreign currency to achieve this. Normally, both loans stand separately, hence the problem of not being able to offset the one against the other.

Parallel loans

Long-dated forward contracts again have the same effect, except that settlement (and, therefore, the hedging) takes place some time in the future, rather than matching interest and capital repayments over the life of the transaction, as with a swap. The technique involves initially selling a contract to pay the foreign currency and then buying it back at an agreed future date. If the foreign currency has moved against sterling in the meantime, the gain or loss on the contract is matched by an equal and opposite gain or loss on the principal loan.

Long-dated forward contracts

Management issues

Once the deal is completed, unless previously agreed, comprehensive management changes are generally to be avoided. Most companies do feel the need both to be seen to take control and to emphasise the change of ownership to local employees. It is not usually necessary to replace the chief executive of the acquired company to achieve this objective, although he will often be one of the vendors of the business and may be eager to leave once he has been paid for his interest in the company. Indeed, the motivation of vendor-managers must be carefully considered. As they may no longer be dependent on the business for their livelihood, many acquiring companies insist on an incentivised earn-out arrangement, with the vendor-managers only obtaining part of the consideration for their shares if profit targets are achieved for a period following the acquisition. In such an event it will be essential to agree in every detail the basis on which the earn-out is calculated if subsequent litigation is to be avoided. In view of the inconsistency of Continental accounting and audit practices, it may, moreover, prove difficult to establish a comparable historic basis on which to calculate an earn-out formula. There is also the risk that the vendor-manager will seek to maximise profits during the earn-out period at the expense of longer term benefits to the company.

Earn-outs

If, however, it is decided to remove vendor-managers, this can hardly be left until after the acquisition, as their contracts of employment are bound to be a feature of the negotiations. Raising the issue early in the negotiations can indeed be helpful, as the selling of their interest in the business can be comprehensively dealt with, including their interest as employees.

But most acquiring companies are satisfied to retain the existing management provided they take immediate control of the finances after the acquisition. Some also make a point of injecting some of their own personnel at one management level or another, in order to instil the group way of doing things and ensure a measure of accurate reporting back to head office.

Removing uncertainties

At some point, direct contact needs to be made with employees other than any owner-managers. Change of ownership is often traumatic for company employees, particularly senior management whose careers become uncertain. It is desirable to remove as much of this uncertainty as possible, as it can lead to difficulties in the management of the business, both during negotiations and in the transitional period following the acquisition. Customers and suppliers need reassurance and, while statements by the acquiring company can occasionally be made publicly in advance of completing the acquisition, a far more effective method of offering reassurance is for the incumbent management to display confidence in the future directly. To be able to do this, they need to understand the nature and intentions of the acquiring company, not just with regard to their own employment.

It is usually possible to draft service contracts for key managers ahead of completion. This is not only reassuring for the managers involved, but also establishes continuity of management during the critical stage for the new owner. Managers will be concerned about continuing their pension arrangements and bonuses and it may be possible to add incentive bonus packages linked to profitability or other measures of performance. Where certain employees are critical to the future of the business, normally in the service industries and professions, 'golden handcuffs' (contracts binding employees to continue working for the company for an agreed period in exchange for an extra payment) may be offered to ensure both motivation and a period of certainty after the acquisition.

'Golden handcuffs'

It is also useful to give new employees a clear idea of how they fit into the group personnel structure. Opportunities to aspire to higher management levels in the group as a whole can be very encouraging. It may be that the target company – particularly if it is a relatively closely knit family-style business – has no existing personnel procedures. Explaining the acquirer's own procedures and any employee benefits that may apply, such as health insurance, can be a very positive factor in winning the support of the workforce.

Whatever the management changes, it is still important to reinforce the atmosphere of a new beginning. Idiosyncratic practices should only be retained when a real value can be attributed to them. Acquiring companies often seek to recruit new senior managers for the acquired company from outside sources. This not only has the benefit of emphasising a new management style, but also reduces the dependence on temporary UK-based managers who may be neglecting other responsibilities. Specifically selected personnel with experience in the relevant market can be introduced, and they will have a direct relationship with the acquiring company and no carry-over of any inconsistent attitudes in the acquired company.

Redundancies and closures

Where redundancies and plant closures are required, there are no easy answers. It is important to avoid the appearance of being asset strippers; at the same time there is no point in compromising the aims of the acquisition by failing to take decisions that may be uncomfortable. Foreign acquirers are often looked on suspiciously, especially if they have no track record of good employment practices in the territory. But there should be a convincing story to tell: some redundancies imposed by the acquiring company may be the only alternative to bankruptcy of the business standing alone. For example, in the acquisition of Patrick, Grampian was able to exclude plants and employees that it did not want from the deal, because it was buying a bankrupt company from the receiver.

Handling industrial relations

A company seeking to establish itself on the Continent needs to be aware of the varying practices of industrial relations and the different requirements of national labour laws. Attitudes of UK management to Continental labour practices have undergone a significant shift in the 1980s. In the UK, as a result of reduced trades union power, management attitudes now tend to be more suspicious of Continental industrial relations. They fear that companies establishing a presence on the Continent will find themselves ensnared in bureaucratic and restricting procedures.

In practice, there is no such thing as an identifiable Continental labour relations system. The shape and detail of labour law varies a great deal between member states. For this reason, companies making acquisitions on the Continent must take local legal advice.

Industrial relations practices differ between countries just as much as national labour laws. Table 15 highlights some of the key features of varying industrial relations practices in the member states. Apart from the UK and the Republic of Ireland, the industrial relations systems of the Community broadly break down into the so-called consensus model of the north (excluding France) and conflict model of the south (mainly Italy and France). In Spain and Portugal, newly emergent democracies, the role of the trades union is different again.

Consensus model
The consensus model is where trades unions are accepted as social partners and employees enjoy legal rights to information, consultation and participation (and, in West Germany, co-determination). In West Germany in particular, the unions are organised on an industry basis, which leads to industry-wide agreements. Unlike the UK, in the northern European systems there is little collective bargaining, formal or informal, at shop floor or plant level. But there is a system of statutory works councils, in which unions tend to play a leading role. The powers and effectiveness of works councils vary considerably between countries, companies and types of establishment.

Works councils have a spectrum of rights to information, consultation and participation. For instance, in the Netherlands, councils have the right to a regular oral report on the order book and employment position and annual written reports on matters such as recruitment, remuneration, training, promotions and dismissals. The German and Belgian systems specify obligatory information requirements in even greater detail. However, in all these countries the disclosure requirements to councils are balanced by confidentiality obligations on the representatives.

Rights to consultations also vary in both scope and practical significance. In Belgium, for example, councils must be consulted on questions of collective redundancies and working conditions. In West Germany, the rights extend to the planning of factories and safety regulations; and in the Netherlands to mergers, new trading arrangements and substantial changes in activity.

Where issues are subject to participation (in the Netherlands this includes rules on hours, holidays, pensions, profit-sharing and safety) the council in effect has a right of veto. In West Germany, participation rights include mergers and dismissals. In the coal, iron and steel sectors, and in very large companies generally, these rights are formalised into a system of co-determination (*Mitbestimmung*). Although shareholder and management representatives retain, in practice, a small majority on supervisory boards (which appoint the management boards), the pressures to proceed by consensus with employees which co-determination creates are widely acknowledged to be overwhelming.

Conflict model

Statutory rights to employee participation are also a feature of French and Italian labour practice. However, they have not created the relatively harmonious industrial relations seen in northern Europe, partly because of the unions' unwillingness to be tied into a consensus framework and because of deep ideological, and even religious, differences between the unions themselves. In France and Italy, there is little union interference with management discretion at company and plant level, although the unions have established a powerful position in some mass production companies and in public services. This approach contrasts with the institutional emphasis of northern European industrial relations.

In Spain, union membership is exceedingly high. The unions have a high degree of moral authority which exceeds their industrial muscle. This is well illustrated in De La Rue's acquisition of the Basque printing firm, Lerchundi. The role of the unions was crucial – both in persuading the proprietors to initiate serious negotiations and in sustaining their commitment when a major fire at the plant threatened the whole deal.

Understanding the distinctive characteristics of the industrial relations system in any EC country is, therefore, clearly important. The role of trades unions may be significant, but there is no reason for it to pose an insurmountable obstacle to the successful pursuit of a European acquisition strategy.

Necessary commitment

Buying an overseas business can be a very long haul. Finding the right acquisition in the first place can take years of perseverance, particularly if the acquisition criteria are demanding.

Table 15: Industrial relations in selected member states				
Countries	% of trades union membership of working population	Union membership compulsory	Works council	Division of unions
Belgium	75%	No	Mandatory if over 100 employees. Consultative body with right to information; no right of veto	Industry-wide trade unions which form 3 multitrade confederations on political lines
Denmark	Most hourly paid workers; many salaried employees	No, although closed shops are becoming a feature of collective agreements	No	Organised by trade
France	less than 20%	No	No	Organised by industry. There may be several unions in each place of work, as each confederation has a different ideological outlook – though not formally linked with political parties
Italy	50% approx.	No	No legal requirement, but a workers' committee is usually established	Organised by industry and politics
Netherlands	25–30%	No – except in printing and allied industries	Yes: every enterprise with more than 35 employees must establish a works council which must be consulted on matters including mergers, set-up or closure of business, employment policies. No power of veto	Organised by industry or trade sector – trade confederations on religious lines

Table 15   *continued*

Countries	% of trades union membership of working population	Union membership compulsory	Works council	Division of unions
Portugal	Nearly 100%	No	Yes	Political
Spain	nearly 100%	No – but there are closed shops in practice	More than 50 employees require a company committee. For mergers etc. the committee must report before action is taken	2 major unions; most unions have nationalist sympathies
UK	50% approx.	No	No	A varied pattern based on historical development of craft, general and occupational unions
West Germany	42%	No	Mandatory if more than 20 employees. General right to information on prospects and financial standing of the employer. Right to be heard on reorganisation and intended dismissals	Organised by industry

A major commitment is needed to carry through a Continental acquisition, including:

- Time and resources for negotiating the acquisition
- A public commitment to the acquired business

Once a target is identified, it can take many months to negotiate the acquisition and can require the continual presence of senior management from the acquiring company, as well as advisers. Following the acquisition, it will typically be necessary to undertake a major review of the acquired company's operational practices. In particular it is essential that firm financial control is taken immediately and that clear reporting lines are instituted. Again, this will usually require frequent attendance by senior managers of the acquiring company, particularly finance executives.

Efforts will have to be made to fill management vacancies and, as these will often be locally recruited, further resources on the ground will be required to find suitable candidates. In the case of turn-round acquisitions, there will inevitably be a demand for more management attention. Deficiencies in the incumbent management must be identified and corrected. It may be necessary to commit management teams from head office for a prolonged period.

Where an acquisition is intended to be integrated into the group as a whole, rather than left as an autonomous unit, efforts will have to be made to transfer technological, marketing and other practices to the acquired company and perhaps vice versa. If the acquisition is significant, there may be a need for a commitment within the group to language training to achieve the best possible relationship with the new business and employees.

Once an acquisition has been made in a new territory, it may well be part of the strategy to bolt on further acquisitions, building on the newly acquired base. This, too, may require senior management involvement – perhaps a director dedicated to the handling of this strategy.

Suppliers, customers and creditors

Beyond this is the need to demonstrate a public commitment to the acquired business. In the first instance, it will be necessary immediately the acquisition has been completed to contact all suppliers, customers and creditors to apprise them of the new situation and reassure them as appropriate. It is normal to prepare a standard letter for most of these, but important trading arrangements should be dealt with by telephone or face to face. This is, in any event, a good opportunity to put over the appropriate marketing message regarding the acquisition to the key people in the market, including statements to the press and opinion formers generally.

In the case of finance, it is essential to ensure that necessary funding arrangements will be in place after the acquisition has been completed. Typically, current account facilities may be taken over, although the lender may stipulate different terms reflecting a changed perception of the risk. It may frequently seek the guarantee of the acquiring company's UK bankers. Creditors will also need reassurance.

Longer-term arrangements are often refinanced, but this is by no means essential. Secured loans over specified properties are commonly left in place, at least initially, until there has been time to review the acquired company's financing needs in detail. Some loans, however, may be repayable immediately as a direct result of the change of ownership of the company. These issues will all need to be researched in advance and it is advisable to to have finance available on a stand-by basis to cover any unforeseen needs.

Fiscal authorities

Arrangements will additionally have to be made with the various authorities in the country, particularly the fiscal authorities. The acquisition may also have to be notified to one or more regulatory bodies, depending on its nature and the country concerned.

This is by no means an exhaustive analysis. It highlights important areas and demonstrates the complexity and ramifications of making an acquisition abroad. Each case will be different; but in every case considerable commitment is required by the acquiring company, and good advice is necessary at every stage. In a nutshell the key ingredients for making successful acquisitions on the continent are careful preparation, endless patience and a willingness to persist.

CASE STUDY

Grampian Holdings
Acquiring brands and distribution

Report of an interview with Nigel Penny, Chairman of the Sporting Goods Division

Grampian is a Glasgow-based holding company with interests in sporting goods, road haulage, knitwear retailing and veterinary pharmaceuticals.

The Sporting Goods Division trades under several famous brand names, the two biggest being Mitre and Patrick, the latter acquired in 1987. The Mitre sports balls business is extremely profitable and the firm's products are used at world class level (the World Cup rugby ball last year, for example) and it has a long-standing sports shoe business.

Nigel Penny sees 1992 as having two major implications for this division. First, with international brand names like Patrick, Mitre, Daiwa Gold and Penfold Golf, the single market will mean that Grampian's brand names are going to play a vital role in spearheading the group's international growth. Second – and this applies to all producers of consumer goods – once barriers come down, local distributors are going to face more intense competition. The trend to EC-wide rationalisation of value added tax and border paperwork will inevitably lead to price approximation. This, in turn, will trigger greater parallel importing and cross-border retailing. 'In the golf business, for example, UK dealers are setting up on the Continent and local distributors are being squeezed.'

Nigel Penny anticipates a greater use of commission agents – along the lines of Patrick's distribution network in West Germany. Grampian's approach to such changes is still being decided, but Penny doesn't rule out the possibility one day of a major, centralised warehouse in Europe, perhaps in northern France, from which Grampian would itself distribute its sports products to European customers.

When Patrick, the French sports shoe and clothing manufacturer, went into receivership, Grampian immediately identified Patrick's sports shoe products as an ideal acquisition opportunity. Nigel Penny summarised his feelings at the time: 'Patrick's shoes had style, flair, were of a high quality and were French!' Moreover, Patrick's interests in sports clothing and its US subsidiaries made it even more attractive.

This acquisition has allowed Grampian to expand its European sales which, although good in the Netherlands and Belgium before the acquisition, were weak elsewhere. Patrick has sales throughout Europe and is particularly strong (not surprisingly) in France. And the US subsidiary, based in California, complements Mitre's US shoe business well.

Patrick was a family-owned business which despite its high margins and profitability suffered from lack of financial control and this finally led the firm into receivership. 'The family had poured money into pet production projects, and had ignored the effect on cash flow. It certainly had an excellent production facility.'

Buying from a French receiver was an interesting experience. The whole process was conducted under the auspices of a regional commercial court, and the receiver had wide powers, 'rather like a US Chapter 11 situation'. His main interest was in protecting the employees, rather than the creditors.

The auction process was very open and rapid – it was all over in two months. There were other suitors – Bernard Tapie, the French corporate raider and Lee Cooper (now called Vivat Holdings), the Anglo-French clothing manufacturer. From the first day of receivership on 15 September 1987, the contenders had until 6 November 1987 to prepare and submit a detailed business plan. The court specified that the plan had to contain a three-year forecast, management plans, the proposed number of employees to be retained and how the deal was to be financed, among many other things. A copy had to be sent to the court, the unions and workers' associations, the receiver, and the owning family. Inevitably, most of the details got into the local press. The price was a secondary consideration to the effect on employment, but Grampian's bid was the highest. The plan was not legally binding, but Grampian nevertheless included a 10 per cent leeway clause concerning the number of employees post acquisition.

Despite the other bidders 'manoeuvring like hell', the press was more favourable towards Grampian and respected its experience in shoe manufacturing. The unions also chose Grampian, as did the incumbent management.

Because Patrick was an important local employer and its finances were in such a bad state, the receiver allowed Grampian effectively to lease the assets until all the liens over them were sorted out, subject only to Grampian committing to purchase them at the agreed price free from all charges. This meant that the business was able to continue without problems from creditors. In fact, Grampian was able to cherry-pick those assets and employees it wanted to take, and has no legal liabilities for any pre-acquisition claims.

Pitching a price was difficult, especially as further working capital would have to be injected. But, because the asset register was in fairly good order, this gave a clear benchmark to work from. Again the support of the incumbent management was vital in interpreting the accounts. The operating accounts were very unsatisfactory although Penny was told by Arthur Young that in fact Patrick's accounts were better than most French accounts! Without the management's support, Grampian would not have been able to get hold of all the figures it wanted – certainly not within the time-scale set by the court.

Apart from finance, the rest of the incumbent management was of good quality and Grampian saw no reason to upset the team. Their retention was a pre-condition to making the acquisition at all. Also, the French unions would have caused problems and the prospect of trying to solve labour problems in France from head office in Glasgow was totally impractical. The finance director for the sports division initially had to spend three or four days a week in France and Penny himself goes over once or twice a month to meet with the local management team.

Nigel Penny has several requirements before going ahead with a European acquisition.

- First and foremost, quality advice is essential. Without this, Grampian would not have gone beyond the first stage of the acquisition, indeed it could not have done so even if it had wanted to.

- Good local management is important. Trying to find new personnel who can cope with local unions and at the same time be appropriately skilled would cause huge problems.

- The cooperation of both local management and the unions is also essential. To some extent, the two go hand in hand, but both are vital for providing information about the company and also for avoiding any untoward complications.

Penny sees Europe as a 'Number one opportunity' and, following the acquisition of Patrick, looks forward to expanding Grampian's sales of sports products throughout the Continent.

CASE STUDY

Dawson International
Bloodied but unbowed

Report of an interview with John Waterton, Corporate Affairs Director

Dawson International is in the business of supplying high-quality knitwear and yarn products to the world – products of 'unashamed luxury', as John Waterton describes them. Dawson is determined that its products should be the best of their kind available. It has always been a strong exporting company. 'The logic of this is simple. There is no way we could find a big enough market solely within the UK for the kind of products we sell.' The targets are consumers with high disposable incomes in the richest countries in the world – mainly Switzerland, Italy, Japan, the USA, West Germany and France, as well as the UK.

Dawson has traditionally been a UK manufacturer with a very heavy emphasis on exports, direct and indirect. For instance, 80 per cent of Dawson's knitwear sold in the UK is purchased by foreign tourists, while 70 per cent of all UK knitwear production is directly exported.

Dawson is, then, by its nature a company that has to think in terms of world markets in which Continental Europe is of major importance. But it was not until the 1980s that it looked at acquisition overseas as well as export.

John Waterton describes how, when Ronald Miller took over as chairman in October 1982, the company made a strategic decision 'to make a reality of the International in our name'. Overseas acquisitions are seen as an essential means of controlling marketing destiny. The company has successfully built up its business in the USA by acquisition. This now accounts for about 30 per cent of turnover and profits. But finding the right acquisition in Europe has proved a more difficult proposition.

When Dawson decided to go for an acquisition strategy, it adopted five main criteria for examining potential prospects:

● Would the acquisition bring Dawson nearer its final customer?

● Had it a healthy track record?

● Did the management of the target company want to stay in place and remain committed to running the business?

- Were there good prospects for growth?

- Was the local management of the company to be acquired a willing member of an international group seeing itself as enriching Dawson's worldwide growth?

It was with these criteria in mind that Dawson saw an early opportunity and decided to purchase KSW in West Germany in 1983. The KSW spinning factory produced two types of product. A fifth of the business was focused on the 'Tuffi' bath mat with a strong brand reputation. The remainder produced hand-knitting yarn.

Only 5 per cent of the hand-knitting output was branded: much of it was 'own branded' by the principal West German retailers. However, the potential to increase the high-margin branded share of the market seemed at the time large, as long as the necessary marketing effort was made. The profit potential in switching a relatively small proportion of KSW's output from non-branded to branded sales looked enormous.

Dawson had purchased KSW at what seemed a reasonable price. Indeed the effect of the takeover was to increase Dawson's earnings per share in the year of purchase. The managing director of KSW seemed an ideal partner. He had been known personally to Dawson management for some time. He spoke English fluently and was committed to continuing to run KSW, which Dawson regarded as crucial. He owned 10 per cent of the business and had been keen on the Dawson takeover because the principal shareholder in KSW, who owned the remaining 90 per cent of the business, had been reluctant to make the necessary continuing investment in the business.

Although the deal took seven months to tie up, mainly because of the need for a large number of warranties, the new subsidiary started well. KSW's main market for hand-knitting yarn was buoyant at the time. The marketing investment was made and KSW pushed up its share of the hand-knitting yarn market in West Germany.

None the less these hopes were not fulfilled, as Dawson, with the disposal of KSW now completed, now acknowledges. John Waterton frankly describes the whole experience thus: 'Far from being our bridgehead on the continent, with KSW we found ourselves on the beach at Dunkirk.'

Two factors were at the root of the problem. First, KSW's main market collapsed. As a result of a change in fashion, sales of hand-knitting yarn have fallen 40 per cent from their peak. But, as John Waterton acknowledges, on a long-term view the market will eventually turn around. The second and fundamental reason for Dawson's disillusion is that KSW proved unable to act as the spearhead for Dawson's continental ambitions.

Dawson had been very anxious that KSW should enlarge on its strong bath mat brand with the acquisition of related bathroom furnishing businesses – principally shower curtains and plastic bathroom accessories. With these acquisitions Dawson would have been able to develop an attractive marketing package, as it has in the USA, targeted at store buyers from the big retail chains. But KSW had proved incapable of taking this step. At root, according to John Waterton, this was due to 'a narrowness of vision – an ability to manage only what one can immediately see, not seize new concepts'.

Other businesses might well have tackled this problem by putting their own management into the subsidiary. But Dawson does not believe in this philosophy. It does not see itself as having the managerial resources at the centre to allocate around what is a highly decentralised group of businesses. Hence the decision to withdraw from KSW.

However, Dawson remains committed to a Continental European strategy. As John Waterton emphasises, 'We are withdrawing with every intention of going back.' Dawson is currently reviewing its own structure and strategic plans. It wants to do more to exploit 'its unique image in the fashion business'. It recognises that it needs to take advantage of the considerable potential for Eurobranding in the field in which it operates. It intends to build on the considerable strength of its knitwear labels (such as Pringle and Ballantyne) in order to create full-scale apparel brands. There are plenty of precedents to be emulated whether British, French or Italian.

One clear route forward is for Dawson to expand its network of shops in wealthy Continental centres. The purpose is not to establish its own retail chain as, for example, Benetton has done by creating some 4,000 franchises throughout Europe. Dawson's strength is that some 15,000 retailers stock its brands. But a select network of demonstration stores could do much to heighten the presence of key Dawson brands, and enable it to market 'apparel concepts' around its established brands. To the extent that this is successful, there could be production economies in enabling Dawson to reduce the number of variants of the basic brands it presently supplies. For example, Pringle currently produces some 55,000 variants per season: but any single store probably stocks no more than 500.

Dawson still sees potential for further acquisitions on the Continent. But as John Waterton admits, 'It is difficult to find suitable businesses we really want to buy on the Continent. The contrast with the United States is striking and there's great potential for joint ventures in Japan.' Asked to explain this contrasting experience, John Waterton puts greatest weight on personality. In the USA, Dawson had identified an individual on the spot who has played a big part in identifying acquisition targets and then managing them if necessary. 'In a small kind of way, he's our Gordon White – Hanson Trust's US mastermind; we've no equivalent to him on the Continent.' Company search on the Continent is therefore a major problem.

On a more general note, John Waterton points to the logic of exchange rate stability as part of a successful European strategy. 'Dawson's products are not exchange rate price-sensitive. We fix our prices in local currencies according to market conditions. But there is a hell of a cost in managing currency exposures'. Fears of a United States of Europe were in his view misplaced: 'What's so wrong with the Swiss model – fierce local pride and independence for each canton, together with acceptance of four separate languages, but within the framework of a common currency and free trading area?'

CASE STUDY

Emess
Mixed experiences in trying to acquire listed companies

Report of an interview with David Cutler, Finance Director

Emess is a company that has enjoyed spectacular growth in the 1980s. It is principally in the lighting business, although its Tenby subsidiary specialises in electrical accessories. Until quite recently its activities have centred mainly on the UK.

Emess has considerable strength in two lighting markets:

- Commercial lighting, where Emess products are sold through contractors and wholesalers having been specified for big building contracts by architects, civil engineers, and developers

- The retail decorative lighting market, where Emess sells through the principal High Street stores and household goods chains and DIY superstores such as B&Q

The decorative retail business is, as David Cutler describes it, a highly competitive business with great concentration on costs. Emess presently enjoys a 12 to 15 per cent share at the high value-added end, but it considers that further attempts to increase market share in the UK will intensify the competition.

Emess has no desire to become a mini-conglomerate. 'We want to remain focused on the industries we know and where we believe we can add value'. That is why Emess decided that further major expansion had to be in non-UK markets, such as Europe. This decision predated the current 1992 debate by two years and was arrived at through Emess's strategic requirement for European distribution, coupled with economies of scale, design and manufacture. A profitable Danish subsidiary was already in place.

In design terms, the lighting business is led by the Italians: 'They tend to be market leaders in design flair.' Innovative designs have a shelf life of about two to three years before they are imitated by a cheap mass producer. But despite the Italian design pre-eminence, the West German market is the most attractive on the Continent. This was the market targeted by Emess.

'The West Germans spend more per head on domestic lighting than anyone else and their products are of much higher perceived manufacturing quality than in other countries. Our own actual quality is at least as high.' Although there is a discernible trend towards greater uniformity in European taste, the national markets are still segmented by important cultural differences. For that reason there were clear limits to the extent Emess could expand in West Germany by direct export, without a strong local distribution chain, while greenfield entry was clearly much more hazardous than acquisition of a going concern, if that could be achieved.

Emess had fixed on BrillantLeuchten of Bremen as the ideal West German acquisition some two years before they got together. 'It took perseverance,' says David Cutler. Emess had had very little contact with the company before negotiations actually opened for them to acquire a stake. BrillantLeuchten had been known through a small-scale trading relationship. But it had a strong reputation as a market leader in West Germany.

Emess decided not to make a direct approach. 'Eventually it was through a German bank that we got in touch with the controllers of the company.'

BrillantLeuchten is a quoted company. This was a factor of some significance in the successful completion of the acquisition, as we shall see. However, 70 per cent of the shares were in three pairs of hands. A 25 per cent stake was divided equally between the husband and wife team who were among the founders of the company and still ran it. The other 45 per cent was owned by a German businessman (who was also the non-executive chairman) who stayed in the background during the negotiations but (it later emerged) was prepared to realise his stake in the company.

The initial discussions were not easy. As David Cutler put it, 'We were told quite firmly that control was not available. We decided to go down the route of a minority stake and build a relationship.'

The decision to be content with a minority stake was, David Cutler admits, a bit of a risk. Although Emess had a high regard for BrillantLeuchten's products, cost controls appeared inadequate and margins were slowly being eroded despite a continued increase in sales. Emess was able, on taking a minority stake, to put a director of its own on the supervisory board. But, managerially, Emess was unable 'to exercise the degree of control on which we would normally insist'.

However the risk was minimised by two factors. First, although the vendors had been prepared to sell Emess no more than a 24.9 per cent stake in the company – below the 25 per cent which in West German law gives minority shareholders important blocking powers – this was a restriction in form rather than substance. Because BrillantLeuchten was quoted, there was nothing to stop Emess buying additional shares on the open market in order to gain the necessary blocking power. Its owners knew this was the position and therefore behaved as though the minority stake gave Emess an effective veto over financial or organisational change.

Second, Emess felt it had a secure exit route if the relationship were to be terminated. 'We took informal soundings with West German banks. Because BrillantLeuchten was quoted, they assured us we would be able to get our investment back through the market.'

Despite the uncertainties, Emess made every effort to win the confidence of the BrillantLeuchten people. 'We worked together to achieve a partnership with a view to ultimately buying them out when mutually agreeable.' The union representatives on the supervisory board observed the development and raised no objections. The company gained an immediate sales benefit through more effective marketing of BrillantLeuchten in the UK. Also it was of considerable help that Peter McGrath, the Emess Vice-Chairman, spoke German fluently, having had experience as an executive of Ford in Cologne many years before.

This successful winning of confidence meant that, within a year, Emess was able to acquire the controlling stake when the founding husband and wife decided to withdraw from active management of the business and to concentrate on design and product development. They recruited a new West German managing director with Emess's full approval. 'They wouldn't necessarily have sold to us, just because we had a minority. They told us it was because of the excellent working relationship we had built up.'

Continuity is preserved because one of the former proprietors is to be chairman of the supervisory board (on which under West German law the managing director is not allowed to sit) and they are both retained as consultants for design and marketing. A very happy arrangement for all.

At present there are only 15 per cent of BrillantLeuchten shares left on the West German market. One curiosity of West German stock exchange practice is the absence of UK- or US-style protection for minorities. Emess paid the principal owners a higher price than was quoted on the market. However, Emess has not sought to exploit this situation, partly because Emess is anxious to maintain the goodwill of the West German stock market should it decide on a further West German acquisition.

The purchase of BrillantLeuchten was financed originally by borrowing Deutschemarks in London from West German banks in order to hedge the West German asset. The flow of dividends from BrillantLeuchten serviced the DM borrowings. Now that Brillant-

Leuchten is fully controlled, Emess has set up a West German holding company. This is highly efficient given the effective 56 per cent corporation tax rate, as the cost of borrowing can be offset against BrillantLeuchten's profits. Also it enables Emess to take advantage of low West German interest rates and provides an asset hedge as well as a tax-efficient vehicle for further West German acquisitions.

BrillantLeuchten is a key addition to Emess's capabilities on the Continent. Joint marketing and product design strategy are being developed and additionally BrillantLeuchten's contacts in the Far East for sourcing its products are being developed.

BrillantLeuchten however is not a complete answer to Emess's needs on the Continent. Emess wishes to develop links in other countries principally in the commercial market, although, as David Cutler puts it, 'the accounts of potential acquisitions in countries such as Italy are difficult to interpret'. In addition, BrillantLeuchten is only on the edge of the commercial market, so a different strategy is clearly required from the domestic market.

Emess's desire to establish a bigger presence in the Continental commercial lighting market lay behind its abortive bid for Holophane in France, which was ultimately acquired by Thorn–EMI. The market is growing. Marlin, Emess's subsidiary in this field, has built up a market share in the UK and established a good business in the Middle East. But it needs to build up its presence on the Continent ahead of the single market in 1992. The group is determined to be ahead of the field of this connection and has had a successful Danish operation for some years.

The acquisition of Holophane would have given Emess the number two position in the French market with a complementary product fit with Marlin and a distribution opportunity for both companies. That, in David Cutler's view, was why the Holophane management were so much in favour of the Emess bid.

Thorn's motives in the affair were different. Thorn is driven by a need to keep up with the competition, principally Philips and Siemens, in the mass manufacturing business of light bulb production. It needs volume to survive as a competitive producer and one way to maintain volume is by vertically integrating in order to gain control of the light fittings business. In essence, in David Cutler's view, 'Thorn's motives in the Holophane case were defensive whereas ours were offensive. We have no intention of moving into light source manufacture.'

Emess's subsidiary, Marlin, had already entered the French market when Thorn made its bid for Holophane. Marlin has sold products to Holophane's main competition for sometime. 'Frankly Holophane was an opportunistic shot for Emess. Our tactics were excellent and enabled us to achieve control without an auction. We got so far because of our own determination and the success of our advisers in raising an unsecured £80 million for the Emess bid within 72 hours of asking.

The story can be briefly told. It all started when Thorn bid for Holophane in April 1988. Emess immediately entered into discussions with the French lighting company's board, and at the beginning of June launched its own higher bid, backed by irrevocable acceptances representing 57 per cent of Holophane's equity and with Holophane board approval. Emess's purchase was to be funded partly by a rights issue, which was – as is usual – subject to approval at an Emess EGM at the end of June.

Thorn's advisers immediately latched onto the question of irrevocable acceptances by a French company's shareholders, calling this a 'grey area'. It argued that allowing one bidder to stitch up control in advance damages minority shareholders by preventing them access to a higher bid. Thorn hedged its bets by increasing its offer to 15 per cent above the Emess bid level. Thorn also claimed some support from the Holophane board at a time when the board was recommending the rival bid.

Thorn next obtained a ruling by the French equivalent to our Panel on Takeovers and Mergers (comprising the Paris Stock Exchange, the Finance Ministry and the stock market regulatory authority, the Commission des Opérations de Bourse) that irrevocable acceptances in general, which might block the way to a higher offer, were unacceptable during a bid period. Emess commented that such a statement had no legal force, and proceeded. But it was at this point that French officials pointed out that, as the Emess offer was conditional on its shareholders approving the rights issue at the end of June, it could not be officially registered by the Stock Exchange. As David Cutler later commented 'the French fiduciary position is geared to 1892, not 1992'.

The next piece of action came when it was announced that the French Treasury had cleared the Emess offer, but the Paris Stock Exchange had refused to register it notwithstanding the fact that Emess now had irrevocable commitments from a majority of its own shareholders to vote in favour of the rights issue. It did, however, clear the Thorn offer. This was the first time the Stock Exchange had registered a later offer (the increased Thorn bid) before an earlier one, and it gave no reason for it. Emess immediately sued the Stock Exchange. This was also a first for the Paris Bourse.

At the end of June, while the litigation was pending, the Emess EGM duly approved the rights issue. Holophane's shares had been suspended until the courts made a decision. The takeover timetable was also suspended.

In the following month the court rejected Emess's appeal, and Emess allowed its bid to lapse. A statement was issued by Emess which commented on the fact that the French authorities had blocked a recommended bid, irrevocably backed by a majority of the target's shareholders. It added: 'It would appear desirable, notably in the context of 1992, that Bourse rules in the two countries (Britain and France) be harmonised.'

It is interesting to note that the courts never actually ruled on the question of the validity of the irrevocable acceptances – the subject of the initial dispute with the Paris Stock Exchange – but decided against Emess on the basis that Thorn's revised bid, which was higher than the Emess offer, was registered first because the Emess offer was conditional on approval of the rights issue and was therefore invalid until the EGM approval was obtained; and that, under French rules, if Emess wanted to bid at that point, it would have had to top the revised Thorn offer by at least 5 per cent.

But as David Cutler now explains: 'Thorn were determined to obtain Holophane, whatever the cost. Our record demonstrates our commitment to increasing earnings per share. Our valuation of Holophane was tightly costed and we decided it was not commercially sensible to match their increased offer. It was worth more to them than to us.'

The disparity of rules governing acquisitions within the EC is clearly a source of concern. It is ironic that the French company Pernod Ricard successfully argued much the same case as Emess in the Irish Distillers case.

London International Group
Acquiring for market leadership

Report of an interview with David Sadtler, Corporate Strategy Director

For the past seven years, London International has been actively engaged in refocusing its business on a limited number of product areas where it enjoys actual or potential market leadership:

- Family planning, where its condom brands, such as Durex, are world leaders

- Health and beauty aids, where LI has strong positions in major European and North American markets as a result of marketing its products through the same distribution channels as condoms

- Household and industrial gloves, where LI is one of four world players

- Surgical gloves, where LI regards its BIOGEL product as a potential world beater

- Photofinishing, where LI claims to be the largest independent photo processor in the world (other than photo paper and film manufacturers)

Refocusing has involved LI's withdrawal from a wide range of business areas, such as paint brushes and electrical accessories. It has also meant a conscious strategy of expansion through acquisition in the chosen core business areas.

Most of these acquisitions have taken place in Europe (including the UK). LI has not, however, pursued a geographically based European strategy as such: the concentration on Europe has flowed logically from the competitive necessity for LI to consolidate its position in those businesses where it sees market leadership potential. Expanding in Europe has, however, certain practical advantages. It is in the same time zone. It is therefore more feasible to adopt a 'hands-on' management approach.

Condoms are a global business and LI faces strong Far Eastern and US competition. LI's brand strength in Europe is of crucial importance, both in terms of its worldwide competitive position and in enabling it to maintain a large sales force and counter challenges from lesser rivals and new entrants. It is as a result of this leading position in the market that LI has the resources to sustain the R&D which is essential to high-quality product development. It also puts LI in an authoritative position with European standard-setting authorities in order to ensure that no degradation of quality is allowed. This is particularly important in light of the advent of AIDS. Condoms are now seen as life-savers and standards in the industry have been upgraded and tightened accordingly.

LI has maintained its investment in R&D in order to behave as a responsible manufacturer and to protect its position against outside competition. At the same time LI has been able to strengthen its position through acquisition in the continental condom market. By acquiring the Italian manufacturer, HATU-ICO, LI gained control of the only other significant branded high-quality producer in the EC. This move extended LI's existing brand range, and it also strengthened its position in the pharmacy trade in Italy and Spain where HATU-ICO enjoys prominent positions with its sales forces in each country, thereby bringing a better balance to LI's operations in Europe as a whole.

In photofinishing, the main thrust of LI's competitive strategy has been the realisation of economies of scale, which has allowed LI to combine low-cost production with quality and speed of service. In the UK, this has enabled LI to take the lead in driving down prices and countering mail-order competition. On the continent, a two-fold strategy has been adopted. Some of LI's European acquisitions, both in and outside the EC, have been mail order companies. These films are transported to the UK for processing, thereby increasing the throughput of LI's UK photofinishing factories. As a next stage, as full capacity in the UK has been reached, LI has acquired photofinishing plants in Barcelona and Ulster. Each will form the base for further expansion in Spain and in Ireland, respectively.

Surgical gloves is a market where LI has global ambitions. Its BIOGEL starch-free glove is unique and has established a leading position in the UK; there is also great potential for growth on the continent and in the USA. Liberalisation of hospital procurement practices may be of assistance in helping LI to break into continental markets.

As a method of operating, LI prefers to acquire 100 per cent of a company and gain outright control. It is wary of joint ventures. As David Sadtler puts it, 'the trouble with joint ventures is that they often seem to end in court'. However, LI may consider a joint venture if it enables it to become more of a world-class player in, say, the Far East in one of its key businesses. Equally LI sees little point in taking strategic stakes. 'Cross-shareholdings serve little purpose in themselves. If a joint marketing deal makes sense, why not leave it at that?'

As far as making acquisitions is concerned, LI has looked at numerous propositions in the last five or seven years and has seriously considered about fifty. Of these it actually bought twenty-five. The ideas for the successful acquisitions mainly came from its own operating companies who know their own markets well. Key questions in deciding whether to proceed are:

- Does LI feel capable of managing the acquisition effectively?

- Does it have a management team of its own available to help run the newly acquired company? Are they fluent in the local language?

- Can LI quickly impose its own methods of financial control, a crucial factor particularly when dealing with newly acquired private companies where practices and habits might traditionally have been different?

Where LI has decided not to proceed with an acquisition, the reasons more often than not include:

- The inability to identify a suitable manager within its own ranks

- Private owners' unwillingness to give the necessary warranties

- The hidden obligations under local employment laws (for example, when purchasing a firm in receivership, which LI had discovered to be a problem in West Germany)

For advice in completing acquisitions, first-class lawyers are essential: and they need to be locally based and particularly in touch with the labour relations scene. In the case of private companies, it is usually necessary to reassure the owners (who might be paternalistic local employers) that continuity in practice will be maintained: as a result, the pace can be much slower than with UK acquisitions of either private or quoted companies.

Another difficult area is the valuation of the company and the procedures a quoted UK acquirer has to follow. The nature of the legal obligations to employees in different Continental countries has an important bearing on the price to be paid in making a Continental acquisition. In addition, the vendor may need lengthy explanations of why stock exchange circulars need to be written, shareholders' approval sought, and past profits and directors' salaries publicly declared. In the HATU-ICO case, LI had to agree to indemnify the owners against the unlikely eventuality of shareholders' approval not being obtained.

Another delicate matter is how payment for the acquisition should be made: acquirers have to be careful to insist on the full propriety of all their actions and that they expose themselves to no risk of adverse legal claims. As a general rule, shareholders in Continental private companies being acquired want cash, not securities.

LI does not allow considerations concerning the methods of financing acquisitions to determine whether it should proceed. LI applies its own internal cost of capital tests: and then, if the project satisfies that test, seeks to finance it in the most appropriate way.

Conclusion

One of the generally accepted weaknesses of British business in the post-war era has been a tendency to become over-obsessed with the latest fad or fashion. It would be a pity if the present interest in and enthusiasm for 1992 went the way of, say, synergistic diversification and productivity bargaining in the 1960s or management by objectives and employee communication in the 1970s. There is no reason why this should occur if senior management pays heed to the lessons this book has drawn out. First it is important to emphasise that none of the case studies are of companies that are 'in Europe because of 1992'. In most cases they have been building up their presence on the Continent for some time past. All are aware of the importance of 1992. But they rightly see it as a catalyst strengthening existing business trends towards the integration of European markets which have been evident for two decades or more.

Of course, as the book has pointed out, 1992 will have a much sharper direct impact in some sectors than others. These are mainly sectors where the integration of European markets has been held back by artificial technical barriers or the impact of government regulation and intervention. Examples of the former are in food and building materials. Examples of the latter are where markets have remained heavily segmented on national lines, as a result of regulation, as in financial services or where public procurement assumes an overwhelming importance. This occurs in industries as varied as pharmaceuticals, computer systems, power station equipment and telecoms switching gear.

Apart from these specific areas of potential high regulatory impact, 1992 should be regarded as equally important for the psychological momentum it generates, as for any particular detail of the measures it proposes. It is just as important for companies to spend time studying competitor reactions as absorbing the detailed implications of EC regulations. The key economic message of 1992 is that the competitive environment will become more intense: there will be losers as well as winners.

A second general conclusion worth underlining is that the conditions for business success on the Continent are pretty much the same as they are anywhere else. Companies will not grow successfully unless they develop a keen awareness of their strengths. A principal motive for expansion on the Continent, and one which recurs time and again in the case studies, is that companies have preferred to develop the businesses they know and where they feel they can add value, rather than to diversify into areas with which they are less familiar in the UK home market.

In addition, companies that have expanded successfully on the Continent have done so only by making a careful and detailed study of the markets in which they are attempting to compete. They need to have a clear strategy and know what they want to achieve. And when they make an acquisition they need to have worked out in advance how they are going to manage it and what is within their own capabilities.

A third conclusion is that successful strategies for the Continental market are likely to be based on patiently building up a position, rather than dramatic and sudden leaps forward. For one thing, the number of large deals on the Continent is relatively small. This arises from the combination of an industrial structure with far more small companies and a shareholder structure and culture which is inimical to the hostile takeover bid. While there are some signs of change, there is no evidence that this will be dramatic in scale. Strategies of organic growth and piecemeal acquisition are likely to remain the only feasible option for most companies for the foreseeable future.

Fourth, in order to operate successfully on the Continent, UK managers have to recognise that while the Continental approach to business is often different, they should not behave as though they think ours is better. This is particularly true of the processes of making acquisitions. Continental companies put a far heavier emphasis on achieving close personal relations with those with whom they are negotiating. Frequently, as family companies, they are concerned that the tradition they have built up will survive and that paternalistic approaches to their workforce will be maintained. Success in winning their confidence requires time, patience and commitment.

Europe has been open for business for some time. 1992 will make it a lot more open. But the prizes will go to those who have a detailed understanding of the markets, and are prepared to go with the grain of the cultures where they are seeking to enhance their competitive position.

Further reading

Budd, Stanley, *The EEC: A Guide to the Maze*, Kogan Page, 1987

Butt-Philip, Alan, *Implementing the Internal Market: Problems and Prospects*, Royal Institute of International Affairs, 1987

Cecchini, Paolo, *The European Challenge*, Wildwood House, 1988

Commission of the European Communities, *Research on the 'Cost of Non-Europe'*, 1988–9: Executive Summaries of Sixteen Studies (Vol. 1); The Full Studies (Vol. 2)

Department of Trade and Industry, *Towards 1992: An Action Checklist for Business*, 1988

EC Commission White Paper, 'Completing the Internal Market', June 1985

Leonard, Dick, *Pocket Guide to the European Community*, Blackwell, 1988

Padoa-Schioppa, Tomaso, *Efficiency, Stability and Equity: A Strategy for the Evolution of the Economic System of the European Community*, Commission of the European Communities, 1987

Pelkmans, Jacques, and Winters, Alan, *Europe's Domestic Market*, Chatham House Papers 43, Routledge & Kegan Paul, 1988

Index